C000154152

THE MONEY MISTAKES OF MOM AND DAD BY ADAM JONES

Copyright (c) 2019 Adam Jones

DISCLAIMERS

NOT FINANCIAL ADVICE

Please note that the content of this book is for informational purposes only. You should not construe any such information or other material as legal, tax, investment, financial, or other advice. Nothing contained in this book constitutes a solicitation, recommendation, endorsement, or offer by Jones or any third party service provider to buy or sell anything including financial instruments in this or in in any other jurisdiction.

All Content in this book is information of a general nature and does not address the circumstances of any particular individual investment model or product. All examples are for reference only and personal descriptions of events occurred in the life of the author and should only be replicated after consulting a financial advisor.

Nothing in this book constitutes professional and/or financial advice, nor does any information in the book constitute a comprehensive or complete statement of the matters discussed or the law relating thereto. The author is not a fiduciary by virtue of any person's use of or access to the book or Content. You alone assume the sole responsibility of evaluating the merits and risks associated with the use of any information or other Content in this book before making any decisions based on such information or other Content. In exchange for using this book, you agree not to hold the author, its affiliates or any third party service provider liable for any possible claim for damages arising from any decision you make based on information or other Content made available to you through the book.

RISKS OF INVESTING

There are risks associated with investing in securities. Investing in stocks, bonds, exchange traded funds, mutual funds, and money market funds, peer to peer lending involve risk of loss. Loss of principal is possible. Some high risk investments may use leverage, which will accentuate gains & losses. Foreign investing involves special risks, including a greater volatility and political, economic and currency risks and differences in accounting methods. A security's or a firm's past investment performance is not a guarantee or predictor of future investment performance.

FOREWORD

Hi my name is Adam Jones but most people call me AJ1, they call me this because my email address at work is adam.jones1 and my wife shortened it as a nick name (before we got together) and it stuck (even my mother-in-law calls it me!). You may remember me from well, nothing I'm sad to say. I have had brief dabbles in local bands in Birmingham (which I am still in one of them, we're called The Motive), business start-ups, mini entrepreneurial endeavours and had what can only be described as a straightforward relatively boring career in the public, private and third sector which has been a constant throughout all of these endeavours. All of this has taken place since I graduated from Aston University with a Public Policy and Business Degree back in 2002. I got a Desmond if you're interested. That's a 2:2 for everyone else, Tutu get it? What? You don't know who Desmond Tutu is? God now I do feel old. Anyway, I don't have a blog or a podcast, I don't have millions of followers on Facebook, I have an Instagram account where I take pictures of craft beer with about 300 friendly followers and that's about as much as I have done in the world of building a personal brand.

So what the hell am I going to talk to you about in this book? How can I help you? Well let's look at this as an origin story, a prequel to the person I am going to be, a story of how I got to where I'm going to get, while I'm still getting there and before you know me for what I am going to be. Basically, The Wolverine before he was Wolverine bit where you and your family can join my journey to where we all want to be (I think!); financial freedom. Note. I didn't realise how big my ego was until reading back over it, I'm not a super hero like Wolverine. What I am is just an ordinary guy that wants to do something positive for his wife, his children, his parents, his friends and if I still have time the rest of the world, by the way this means you too!

This book is about my personal growth into an adult in the world of money and fiNance. It is where I reflect upon how my parents influenced me and how most of their advice on this topic was debunked over a 4 year period. It's about how I've had to fight against them as well as friends and family to even start the journey of trying to make money and battle against the 'common sense' and widely followed beliefs of the people around me. I'm hoping you will find it useful not only for yourselves to learn the lessons that I did by giving you and your parent's an 'easy' read on these topics. I also share some of the personal stories of where my parent's (mostly incorrect) beliefs came from and the difficulties I've had in convincing them and loved ones that my risk taking is for the good of us all and not just me being a trigger happy gambler. Also, in the spirit of being honest, after all we're going on a little journey into the past together, it's worth letting you know that I was a gambling addict for a couple of years due to some crap that happened in my life. I can tell you first hand that it sucks, it's a serious addiction, in my opinion it is up there with drugs and alcohol but maybe more scarily, unlike those other two it is easily hidden as it doesn't present itself in physical ways. If you think you or someone you know has a problem, please offer help to them. www.gambleaware.co.uk.

Introductions over, the story of this book begins here, I'm lying in a king size bed with a slight hangover in a plush suite (with a Jacuzzi in the room yeah baby!) in Zakynthos which is Zante (Greece) for the uneducated amongst you, don't worry I didn't know until I got here either. Did I mention I was shit at geography? Well I am. Anyway, I'm on my honeymoon with my beautiful wife Claire and I've decided, instead of getting some more needed sleep, to write this book instead. What a trooper? I've also decided to try to get it finished before I go back to work in 9 days' time. Note. This did not happen but I'm pleased I finished it anyway.

So before I get in to the nuts and bolts of this book I need to let you know that my Mom and Dad are awesome people, they've given me the best life and continue to be excellent supportive parents in to my late 30s and their retirement years. We rarely have a cross word and if we do it's usually with my Dad who, I think takes a bit of sport on reading me so called 'facts' from the Daily Mail grrr! Anyway, political pettiness aside, this book is meant to be a semi-serious, slightly autobiographical, tongue in cheek but hopefully helpful trip through mine and my parent's tumultuous life around the topic of money. I should state that they have always worked in full or part time employment for as long as I can remember up until my Dad's retirement at the age of 55 (fair play to him!) and always provided and been generous about money in every way possible towards me, maybe worth sharing that I'm an only child. Don't judge me!

So if you have such awesome successful parents, why are you writing this book and why now you ungrateful bastard? Well, having read a shitload of books on money and watched my folks go through ups and downs over the years with cash flow issues, I feel compelled to write this book as an aide memoir for me (little trip down memory lane) but also a guide for you and your loved ones to a) learn some money rights and wrongs and b) a guide for our folks (my word for parents). This will hopefully show then where they might be going wrong with money matters and help improve everyone's financial situation. All of this wrapped up with a provocative enough title to make you pick it up and buy it. Hopefully not from a bargain bin in Oxfam.

And finally, just before I dive in any further, here is a list of books I've read to get me to this point on my money knowledge
Think and Grow Rich - Napoleon Hill
Money - Rob Moore
How to be F*cking Awesome - Dan Meredith
The Millionaire Mind - T Herv Ecker
The Millionaire Fast Lane – MJ DeMarco
Unshakeable – Tony Robbins
The one minute millionaire – Robert G Allen/ Mark Victor Hansen
(Little Book of) Results - Jamie Smart
Join Me - Danny Wallace
And last but not least, all the Rich Dad Poor Dad books by Robert Kyosaki.

Thanks to the above authors for giving me the tools and tips not only to improve my own financial situation but also to encourage me to try in vein to help my parents with money now they're in their retirement years. Which I can tell you is a rather frustrating task! A big thanks, in particular to Rob Moore, for being an inspiring author and speaker in this field which I'd say has been the biggest influencing factor on me writing this book. I hope this book will do all of these authors justice and inspire people to read their books too. I have a cack memory so all of the stuff I've used from them (unless stated) will probably have come from one or more of the ones mentioned.

Finally and most importantly, thanks to my parents for being cool in general but also for them being as understanding enough to let me publish the anecdotes contained within this book with I must say very little vetoing when proofread by my Mom.

CHAPTER 1
WHAT'S THE
DEAL?

So what's the deal with this book? Bill Gates is reported to have said that if you're born poor it's not your fault but if you die poor it is. That's a pretty powerful quote isn't it? Well I wasn't born poor but I wasn't born rich either although as an only child (and first boy in the whole of my family for ages) I felt like I was rich as I was spoilt by my parents as far back as I can remember. They refused to admit that I was spoilt at the time of my growing up, which I naively believed into early adulthood when they finally came clean and told me that I was really. I bloody knew it!

My Mom; Nette and Dad; Ray aka 'Bastard Face' (coined one night by Mom at a pub quiz) always worked hard and, to be fair to them, they did do some money things right. I would argue that these were the normal things for people of their baby booming generation to do, such as them buying their own home, bonus for me, and Dad had an amazing pension enabling him to retire early, bonus for him. Then why is this book called mistakes? I hear you cry out in wonder? Well, as well as the positive things that they have done in their life together outside of the realm of money e.g. loving each other 40 years plus and my Mom not killing my Dad with a carving knife (I would have!) and of course keeping me alive which was no mean feat, I believe that they could have been so much better off financially if they'd been less risk averse. I also believe that a lot of other people and their parents could have been too and still could be, if it wasn't for many of the money misconceptions cemented into their minds which may have been correct for previous generations but not necessarily the right thing to do in this day and age. I want to help everyone get understand what they can do to be richer and become that superhero that I think I am; Cashman! Lol. Oh yeah I hope you don't mind but I write 'lol' for when I'm laughing at something, usually my own jokes. If you're a parent or someone ahem, slightly older, this means 'laugh out loud' and not as my mom thought; 'lots of love'. By the way, I do know it's not literary prowess to write lol but it's more me that 'haha' and to be fair I'm not looking to win any literary awards, just your hearts, vomit.

My theory is that the circumstances that they and others were born into and then subsequently experienced (post-war rationing, market crashes, strikes and recessions) taught them to be so frugal that it stunted any chance to be truly wealthy through undertaking more risky investments and the like. My Dad makes me laugh when he talks about the 'good old days', he says that these were a fallacy, he said people used to be able to leave their front door open not because you could trust everyone but because they hadn't got anything to steal. Everybody had the same, if you woke up one morning and you had three chairs and your neighbour had five you knew who'd had it. Lol. Where was I? Oh yes and the other theory which I hold is that the world is a different place, not a Gary Glitter alright in the 70s different but not now type of place. But the things that made money back then, hard work, graft having a trade etc. are no longer what is likely to make you loads of dosh (bet you haven't heard that word for a while). Don't get me wrong, trades and manual work will put a roof over your head yes but these have now been replaced with the digital age, computers, internet and programming which have all paved the way to earn cash simpler, smarter and quicker.

So here's the kicker, my folks' money beliefs from their generation influenced my money beliefs which I believed to be true and followed not adjusting for the shift in culture and finance. I think that a lot of people have innocently and incorrectly done this too. Take 5 minutes, to think about where your approach to money comes from, you weren't just born knowing to put your cash in an ISA or whatever, someone has told you and this then shapes your approach for your money matters moving forward. To be fair this would have been fine and probably accurate for previous generations to do as not much changed from generation to generation, but given the massive shift in approach to making money between our two generations (manual to digital), the impact on those that are following their parents misguided beliefs may be lagging behind, if they're in the race at all. Let's face it the apple doesn't really fall too far from the tree does it? I hate to admit it, but I am my Dad and you're probably one or both of your parents, and I see my six year old son picking up my traits every day, some of them to my dismay if I'm completely honest. This is evolutionary, and it is reflective of what happens in the wild, when the older more experienced parents demonstrate to the young what to do so that they can survive like they have, this is called imprinting. The only problem is that animals haven't got the internet, so it is ok for them to keep repeating the lessons down through the generations whereas our parents hadn't even heard of the term online let alone online banking so how could they teach us about this new technology? The answer is they couldn't, instead we had to learn it and teach it to them, which I'm sure you can agree is a bit awkward. Imagine a lion cub teaching his Dad to hunt for deer thanks to new technology in teeth or something, not pleasant for either party. The older one thinking who's this upstart telling me how to survive and the young one thinking is it really my place to be doing this at such a young age. Bringing it back from the animal kingdom, our parents have to learn to trust us to help them but by the same token we need to respect where they're coming from and what they've achieved so far.

So my life and my relationship with money reflected my parents' up until about the age of about 34ish. This was until I was recommended Cash Flow Quadrant by Rich Dad Poor Dad; Robert Kyosaki by my friend and business partner Chris. From the moment I read the first chapter I was hooked! It introduced me to totally new concepts that I'd never seen or heard before but it made total sense once my eyes were open to them, it was like waking up from a coma, a coma of what not to do about money. I started inhaling all of these 'secrets' of the successful that until now had been hidden in plain sight and started to read even more books along similar themes. And it was round about this time when I realised we (the Jones's) had been going about money all wrong and so had many of my family and friends. But I only worked out that the 'mistakes' I was making were primarily to do with my folks and their life influences recently when they sold our family home to, in their words, let me have my inheritance while they're still alive. See told you they were ace! But also to give them a nest egg until they pop their clogs, which I hope won't happen for a long time yet. Our different approaches to our respective pots of money were completely different and in some cases made both of us question each other's financial intelligence. Up until this point their money advice had been passed to me unquestioned and as mentioned they were young in a different time to me with different opportunities and threats and this was becoming more and more apparent because I wanted to maximise the money that they had given me through investments and they wanted to save their money in the bank and in Premium Bonds.

Over the remainder of this book I'm going to cover what I've observed of their behaviour towards money and also that of a few other parental figures I've encountered through my life while growing up through a lens of my new learning and a light hearted dig at them and me, in order to help you understand money and investment principles with some A' Level psychology thrown in for good measure. That'll teach you to wind me up with Daily Mail dross won't it Bastard Face?! Mwhahaha!

At the end of each chapter I'll be popping in a handy 'Mom and Dad think' vs 'reality' just to bring home the key messages. Some of the 'wrong' ways to think weren't my parent's views but for consistency I'll leave that bit as it is even if it wasn't them or state that they didn't think much about it. I'm sure you'll be able to grasp it.

Mom and Dad think: I'm going to embarrass them with this book.

Reality: I wouldn't dream of it!

CHAPTER 2 MOVE YOUR ASSET

As discussed, in spite of the title this book is not really about my parents specifically, this is more about a generation or two that due to so many things happening to them topped with advancements of technology, they have forgotten or maybe never known the secret to making real money, by this I mean over and above what they need to live (food and shelter etc.). The main thing that I think is missing from their knowledge is the process of buying assets and then making money from it which generate something called cash flow, which is the amount of money moving in and out of your accounts and is key to financial success. Cash flow can be generated through renting out property, writing original music, films or books, patenting something or lending people money and charging them interest on the loan. For completeness cash flow can be generated by your salary from your job but even with a healthy bonus reward system in place this will always be capped and involves trading your time for money. For the purposes of this book I won't be discussing increasing your cash flow by earning more money at work as I want you to earn without working. Wahoo!

A good quick example of an asset is, Noddy Holder arguably wrote the best Christmas song ever back in the 70s with 'Merry Christmas Everybody' and now doesn't have to play the song to be earning money from adverts, Spotify and CDs. Can you see what he did? The initial creation; writing the song, involved effort but the money making ability of the song will continue for years to come probably for him and his children and their children too. At Christmas he's literally earning money while he sleeps, and coupled with the rest of Slade's back catalogue he never has to work again, well done Noddy! This is what is known as passive income and is the secret to wealth generation that I have gleaned from the many books I have read and that I want you and your parents to understand too.

NB. Probably worth noting that Noddy isn't that keen on this song after playing/ hearing it so much over the years so if you choose to make money through music, you might be loaded but you might hate the sound of your own voice.

Mom and Dad Think: Nothing about assets or cash flow.

Reality: Without assets or cash flow you trade time

for money and potentially gather debt too.

CHAPTER 3 'JUST DON'T LOSE ALL OF YOUR MONEY'

The title of this chapter is a direct quote from my Mom when I told her I was planning to use some of their gift from the house sale to buy a rental property. 'Don't lose all of your money'. Wow what a thing to say, I shook my head in disbelief and dutifully said 'I won't Mom' like a young boy assuring his mom that he won't get his new trainers muddy. Actually, if you repeat this response in the Harry Enfield 'Kevin and Perry' voice and stick a loud 'MOM!' at the end of it you can probably relate to it even more. Now I know what you're thinking, I'm being a bit harsh and ungrateful as all parents worry about their kids, from their first trip going out into town on their own, to passing their driving test and getting behind the wheel of a car for the first time, to drinking too much on their first night out. But I'm 38 years old for god's sake and have been a professional with a degree for 16 of those years, plus being a parent myself and now being married, all of this time I haven't died or having to live on the streets. I did break my leg from jumping out of a second story window but I learnt my lesson and also got the World Cup off work, so every cloud!

What was she actually saying by don't lose it', seems obvious that if I'm given money, I'm not planning to lose it, I'm a reasonably sensible guy, random gambling problem during a dark period several years ago but well and truly put to bed now, so where is this voice of worry coming from? Why does she think I'm going to lose it? Did she actually mean 'don't spend it'? It was at that Moment where she said this that it clicked and there it was my 'eureka moment'. She'd seen money come and go and didn't want mine (that she'd sold the family home for) to do the same. Allegedly, my Nan and Granddad (her Mom and Dad) had been relatively wealthy from a pay out from a work accident that my Granddad had, and according to family folklore, in a bid to be popular spent the majority of this windfall on parties for the street where they lived. This was great for a short period of time but by the time I was born years later, my Nan and Granddad were what I would describe as poor or working class at best. I must stress that this had no impact on me or my parents' relationships with them. They were lovely and it never felt like they were poor when I was growing up, spending many a happy weekend there but essentially they didn't have lots of disposable income to speak of. Basically, if an unexpected payment arrived it could mean a drastic tightening of belts which perhaps could have been avoided if they hadn't 'wasted' the money they had on parties. Was this what my Mom was worried about me blowing my wad on parties for friends? If this was her thinking she definitely had nothing to worry about.

On top of the fact that she had seen money lost or wasted on frivolity, her beliefs were more than likely further compounded with a 'shortfall' in my Mom and Dad's endowment mortgage which left them with a quite a big payment to make up the difference. Then to top it off they witnessed recessions and market crashes plastered all over the news throughout their lives, and Bob's your uncle, Fanny's your aunt - a concerned Mom not wanting to see her son 'lose' his cash. Ok I get it and if that's what she needs to say at the point of handing over a load of money to me then fine. To be fair to my Mom and Dad they haven't tried to influence me too much about where I have to put the money they gave me and I have really tried my best not to say anything too controversial about where they have, in my view wrongly, chosen to put theirs until I wrote this book. Lol. See I can't help myself. What a twat I truly am?!

Now, I don't think my Mom is alone in this thinking, my wife's Mom Hazel also expressed similar concerns when I told her I'd planned to have two mortgages (the second to for a buy to let property) and I'm pretty sure that a lot of the working to middle class British population over say 60 are this risk averse around money because of the financial struggles that they've experienced or seen friends and family bitten by in their own lives. Basically, you can't blame a Mom for being worried, they want their family to survive and thrive long after they've gone - hence why they want us (their children) to marry so we've got someone to look after us when they're not there anymore. In this instance, seeing their son or son-in law about to take on two of something that took them their whole life to pay off, it's understandable that they are slightly worried.

Their money beliefs are understandably different to mine but what's their alternative approach? 'Save your money in the bank and live off it forever?' Personally, I think that notion is as risky if not riskier than property investment, sadly, there are no more 'jobs for life' which they were accustomed to and would make saving up the reasonably sensible option but given the current climate of financial volatility, technology disruption of cryptocurrency, buy to let, zero hours contract job this is not sustainable. Ok if you're pretty good at your job and have a good wage, and if you don't want to earn anything from your money and live off it for a while, on paper it's not riskier but at last check the interest rate on my standard bank account was 0.5%! So in time, with this rate of interest lower than inflation my money being 'saved' is slowly being eaten away by time anyway. Does that count as losing it Mom?

Just to clarify that point about inflation, let's say you've got £10 and you're earning 0.5% per year, next year it will be worth £10.05 (assuming you're not paying tax but you might be). Ok you've made 5p jobs a good un right? Wrong! Inflation has more than likely taken place meaning the cost of the things you spend on have gone up. And let's say it's increased **by 2%** meaning that most things you buy and what your money is relative to will have increased in price. Essentially this is devaluing your cash from the original £10 of last year that you've bravely left there to earn your 5p on. So your original £10 next year in real terms will be worth **£9.85** in today's money. Multiply this by your savings and you can see that you need to stick your money somewhere else.

Mom and Dad think: Put your money in the bank, don't spend it then it'll be 'safe' for when you need it.

Reality: Money in the bank is being eroded slowly by time right from under your nose like a little thief coming in and taking a couple of pence a night thanks to low interest and higher inflation.

CHAPTER 4
YOU DON'T
WANT ANOTHER
MORTGAGE
DO YOU?

Does the above sound familiar to you? Again, this was straight from my Mom's mouth and into my ears (and I should say also echoed by others younger than my parents) when I told them I was contemplating a rental property with my part of the proceeds from my folk's house sale. This is not a 'buy to let' book but I do feel the need to cover the benefits of it in this chapter just in case this knowledge hasn't been imparted to you. Also, I do need to share that, at the time of writing this book, I have not bought a rental property yet but I do intend to do so over the next few months, probably after Brexit has happened and the dust has settled from that whole mess. That reminds me; I better go and buy some tins of beans to hoard in my bunker just in case there's a 'Millennium Bug' style panic.

Anyway, the reason I have decided that I am going to invest in property is because based on what I've read and seen, property seems to be a pretty safe and secure way of putting your money to work and generating cash flow. Buying a property or two and charging rent on it should generate you money long after the initial work and deposit have been paid for and hopefully forgotten. Notice how I said 'put your money to work', as discussed in an earlier, this is something that I think is missing from our financial education at school and wasn't taught to me or my parents either, the concept that money should not just be saved (hoarded) in the bank but put to use, whether invested in to companies, lent to people for interest payments or as I'm about to cover buying either a property or an asset that will either gain in value or that you can charge a fee for its use, maybe even both of these if you're a clever git.

The best way to get a property is to purchase it with a mortgage and rent it out. I know this seems obvious but I just wanted to reiterate this point that if you have a large sum of money to invest in property, and the option is to either buy one outright or get two using mortgages, I would recommend using mortgages. I understand you probably think you should try and own the asset and not have the debt of a mortgage but to generate cash flow the mortgage option gets two lots of income and the rest is of the money is the bank's. Property is appealing to me for this very reason, as you are leveraging your initial deposit that would have probably sat in the bank and earned you about £20 interest per year towards buying something tangible leveraging the bank's money to do so. The Cash Flow Quadrant by Robert Kyosaki states that by purchasing depreciating consumables TVs etc. that don't hold their value we are devaluing our initial pot of money (the principal) what you should be doing is buying things that generate money and appreciate in value. I'll be honest I had never heard of this and it totally amazed me to find out, when I finally did. Rob Moore describes a normal 9 to 5 job as trading time for money whereas property can create 'passive income' where your amount of work is reduced by using assets, and this really resonated with me maybe a little too much as my plan now is to ditch the day job and be a property developer/ entrepreneur. Sorry Mom!

Now as much as buy to let had always seemed like a good idea to me there were a few psychological barriers for me to do so possibly passed to me by my parents. My friend who will be known as X offered to help me buy property back when I started my first job and it just seemed 'too risky' given that I only earned £17.5k per year and was about to buy my own house with my girlfriend at the time. How could I afford another property on top and then the 'hassle' of getting the rent and maintaining boilers and all that boring stuff that you didn't want to be bothered with when there was lukewarm Carling at home to be drank? Needless to say I refused X's offer and when we met back up recently after we lost touch, I cursed the younger me for not having the foresight of 'just getting on with it' like X told me to at the time. However, this is not a tail of regret (I was told that there's no point regretting anything as I must've wanted to do the thing or not do the thing at the time I did or didn't do it) but I do look back through the haze of Carling and vodka and wonder how much of those negative words were my own and how many were my parents, other parental figures that I had in my life at the time and the mainstream media with its doom and gloom outlook for property investment also helped me be risk averse. Either way I chose not to invest and X did and he is now a millionaire and I for shame am not. Sad face emoji (yes I meant to write that and didn't leave it in by accident as I thought it seemed more poignant ok?!).

If you are unaware of why property investment is so good or need more convincing here are a few good reasons why you should stick your money (that you can afford) into buy to let today (or maybe after Brexit just in case!):

1)   You gain an asset that continues to provide you with a revenue stream long after your initial investment has been paid off through the

tenants rent (cash flow).

2)   You use the banks money via a mortgage to gain the property over and above what you have for the deposit, allowing you to own something worth more than you can afford alone, and why some of the authors mentioned in this book call it 'good debt'.

3)   Thanks to the Property Cycle, the value of the property will more than likely go up (see The Complete Guide to Property Investment by Rob Dix) meaning that once it's in your name, inflation that bastard that hinders your savings, actually helps your asset be worth more in case you want to or have a need to sell it in the future.

4)   The rate of return (if you do your maths right and buy wisely) should be considerably higher than the interest that you would earn on a standard bank account, so the rent will cover the mortgage. Thanks tenants!

5)   The property is an asset within your portfolio and in reality safer than depreciating cash in a bank. Also, reassuringly it's a physical object that you can point at and say 'that's mine' which is cool!

6)   If you forego a small amount of the rental income from the property and leverage a lettings agency, after your initial effort from the purchase, your effort to receive the income from the asset is minimal making it potentially passive income.

7) If you're clever and read some of Rob Moore's books there are ways of getting your initial deposit back which means you own these assets without using any of your own money. You should definitely have a read about it as it sounds awesome if you can be arsed to do it!

I think that this aversion to buying property of the previous generations has a few factors but the main one, in my view is because they have been bought up to see all 'debt' as negative. However, thanks to the books I've been reading, this myth has been quashed and I have come to realise that mortgages to buy property can be 'good debt'. This is because this process takes your small amount (deposit), along with the tenants (rent) and the bank's money (mortgage/ loan) to buy something that you may not have been able to afford. The rental income after you take away the mortgage payments then becomes the Holy Grail which is cash flow. I agree it sounds too good to be true but why else would people continue to put their money into property if it wasn't so lucrative?

I attribute this fear of mortgages down to the fact that we/ or our families typically don't take them out very often, if indeed at all. This is possibly due to administration or financial reasons that we become fearful of doing it as it seems quite hard and risky to do so. Most of us don't go to funerals all of the time (thankfully) so when we have to go to them we don't know how to behave, this I think is the same with mortgages. It's not like buying a can of coke (obviously), it's a house where even the cheap ones are quite expensive to most people. There are also loads paperwork and details to check and coupled with the perceived potential to make a loss, I really get this aversion. Also, because most people we know either have one that they probably don't want, and the notion of getting multiple numbers of them can seem absurd or even scary to the majority of society we typically tend to shy away from taking out more than one. It's not just parents that have this view, for instance, I told one of my friends that I was planning to invest some of my windfall into property and in trying to help me he advised me against it and gave me negative stories that he'd witnessed of buy to let. This led me to wonder how much his parents had influenced him as I believe he's from a closer generation to my folks than I am to them, he is very good at saving though so perhaps that's what that generation tend to be good at.

There's probably a new generation of risk-averse parents being created as we speak (or as I write) because of other factors such as global market and property crashes of recent years. I saw a guy (who seemed a bit of a dick anyway to be honest) on Location, Location, Location which is a house buying programme in the UK, and he was reluctant to purchase anything, and I mean anything, just in case there was a property crash and he was left with negative equity like his parents were during the last recession. This is obviously irrational thinking but a vividly real perception for him and I can imagine very frustrating for his partner. If I'm honest, I used to think the same as him and I had similar worries until I read Rob Dix's book who suggests that there will always be crashes and this is part of the property cycle. However, the crashes are always followed by a bounce back higher than before the crash. The key Dix says, is that while the prices are dipping you have to be patient and not sell, which would effectively seal you into the loss, if you are hold its what's known as a 'paper loss'. By being brave and holding strong where possible, there is a good chance the market will recover and you will be rewarded. In other words, fortune favours the brave (and patient).

Funnily enough, I've also noticed that patience seems to be the key for a lot of investments involving risk. I read on a stocks and shares forum the other day regarding paper losses on a share or negative equity on a property that 'you only lose when you sell'. This is so f*cking true but I watch the majority of people (and me in the past) think something is losing value and immediately try to offload it only to be met with a rebound after a period of time has passed. 'Patience, Patience, Patience' should be the name of the show! Think about it if you're offloading it and someone is buying it cheap, they're obviously seeing a bargain that they can capitalise on at a later date, at your expense. Basically, they're using your impatience against you; the phrase I like is that 'the stock market is a way of transferring money from impatient people to patient people'. Think about that for a sec, are you impatient? Who's your money going to when you sell? Me now hopefully haha.

I read somewhere that the reaction to loss is a relatively worse feeling compared to our positive reaction to us gaining something. In other words we feel shitter about losing £10 than we would feel good if we found £10. This is linked to when we were hunter gatherers and basically the loss of a meal (I dunno, our food eaten by some dinosaur or something) was worse from a survival perspective than if we found extra food because the benefit of the extra food would not prolong our life due to it going rotten but the loss of food has instant effect of endangering our odds of survival because we haven't got enough resources to continue living, procreate and invent the Iphone XS. In other words, loss provides a greater emotion than gain does when it comes to our instinct towards food which has transmuted in to money in our current lifestyle where food is in abundance. Well here's the news peeps, there ain't no dinosaurs anymore if you lose some cash you probably won't die although I can't 100% guarantee this, as you might lose someone else's cash and they might kill you. Tough break if that's true but on the whole I think this is right for most people.

Please don't think I am cool as a cucumber when sitting on a loss. I do have to sit there and remind myself to hold and not panic when something I have purchased at a higher price such as a share is losing its value, for this very reason. I will also probably have to do this when property takes a dive during my future buy to let ownership and listen to the Rob Dix audio book on repeat, rocking in the corner, until it's over!

Mom and Dad think: Property investment is risky due to having extra debt in the form of a mortgage.

Reality: A mortgage can be good debt and utilising one or more to purchase property that can be rented out can be a sustainable long term (passive or low effort) income long after the initial deposit has been recovered.

CHAPTER 5 YOU ARE KEEPING SOME FOR A RAINY DAY?

Another quote from my Mom and I'm guessing another common statement amongst her generation and one that resonated and stayed with me from an early age. A rainy day?! Sorry Mom but wtf?! Why do I need money on a rainy day? Surely at the most, I just need the cost of a rain coat, umbrella, a cup of coffee and an Uber home right? So say £250 max and that's with a decent rain coat. Ok I'll save that, now what?

Of course I'm joking, the principle here is fine and what she is suggesting that I should save for when things go wrong and I appreciate that it is prudent to have some cash at hand in case of an emergency. I think it frustrates me because I know my Mom is referring to a massive amount in the thousands of pounds mark. I guess what she's really referring to is injury, illness or loss of a job, a life changing event that could prevent me paying the mortgage or not being able to afford to live or support my family. However, there's one thing my Mom is forgetting here, that we have home insurance, car insurance, breakdown cover and the NHS for most types of those 'rainy days' and in some of those instances, all of the money in the world can't improve the situation unfortunately. It's like money is seen as a safety net but it can only do so much after a few thousand. I'm not saying spend like there's no to-morrow but just check what your thinking is and how much 'just in case' money you are keeping for rainy days.

Also and here's the bit where I go a bit off piste, The Secret, Rob Moore, T Herv Ecker and Napoleon Hill all state that the more you focus on something, whether positive or negative, the more the universe appeases you and gives you what you're focusing on. It thinks that by focusing on it you want it and it dutifully gives it to you. I think the phrase is 'what you focus on expands', this also works the opposite way, so if you don't focus on money you don't get as much by not paying any attention to it. You get the idea. So if your money is for a 'rainy day', what are you going to get? Rainy days! If you say you can't afford something you want, the universe will oblige and guess what? You won't be able to afford it, but if you say you can afford it then the universe gives you what you need and also you probably could have afforded it if you were honest with yourself in the first place. Saving for a rainy day assumes that things have got to be total shit to spend your money, which in your mind at least stops you enjoying your hard earned cash when times are not so hard or perhaps even when they're good. So why not save for a sunny day? See what happens.

Again, I think my parent's thinking came from the scarcity that they were born into that has led them to fear the negative rather than focus on the positive returns from riskier investments. To them, keeping their money as cash in the bank (or probably under the mattress) so they can easily get hold of it for an emergency, feels more secure than tying it up in property or investing it somewhere for higher returns. This would be not as easily accessible to them as cash from the hole in the wall, all the time forgoing higher rewards and inflation doing its worst to them. Imagine if you or I were born into rationing and scarcity, we'd probably have a different outlook on life and when I think about it like that I have empathy for them but I wasn't born into scarcity I was born into abundance, abundance provided by them and lived through even more abundance so I need them to let go of the rainy day mentality even though it helped them get to where they are today. Ironic isn't it?

Please note any burglars reading this, my folk's money is not under their mattress, at least I hope it's not.

I'm not sure how much I buy into the Secret and Law of Attraction but it's quite compelling to think that if you think and talk positively about money it will come to you and if you think and talk negatively about money it is repelled from you. People who I know who've been negative about money and I mean a lot tighter and resentful of others' wealth are usually the ones with the least yet the ones who're grateful and positive about others and generous with it, mostly seem to be better off. Think of the guy you know who avoids getting the round in, how often do people eventually stop getting him a drink or worse, not inviting them out at all? The person who always gets the round in is always offered a drink and invited out. This is another example of where being generous can reap rewards and being stingy reduces the chance of reciprocity down the line. And if you're one of those that don't get a round in, stick your hand in your pocket tightwad! You must like the people you go out with otherwise you wouldn't be out with them. They'll stop inviting you if you don't buy them a drink. If you can't afford a round of drinks then don't go out.

My folks are a mix of the two I'd say, they save for 'rainy days' etc but quite positive for others to do well like if someone has a win on the lottery they'll be pleased for them. If I were to explain my views on this to my Dad I know he'd probably laugh and take the piss a bit so I keep this 'fluffy' stuff to myself. I guess if he reads this he'll have something to say, but equally I'll have something to say back.

Mom and Dad think: Save for a rainy day, you never know when you might need it.

Reality: You get what you focus on, so the more you focus on rainy days the more rainy days you get, so focus on sunny days to spend your money on.

CHAPTER 6 WE'LL STICK TO WHAT WE KNOW

My Mom and Dad love Martin Lewis and so do I, he seems like he genuinely cares about helping people to save money and fair play he's building a successful TV career as well as (probably) many other spin offs while following this passion. My only slight beef with Martin is that his website assumes we need to 'save' money which I believe is a psychologically negative thing to say and do, remember rainy days from the last chapter. I mean who or what are we saving it from and what are we saving it for?

As mentioned in the previous chapter, Napoleon Hill's book Think and Grow Rich advocates that what you focus on manifests more of it, so if you focus and think about saving money and scarcity you will only save money or need to save rather than prospering. My new view since reading all of these wealth books is that we need to invest the money we've saved, thanks to Martin, and we should then invest it. I somehow don't think the British public would go for a show called 'investing expert'. And there lies the rub (weird phrase I know!) the general working/ retired public don't think about investing because to them it's 'too risky'. They'd rather shop around for 1.35% savings account with a high street bank that pays them nothing for being loyal for above 12 months, not only wasting their time for a measly 0.05% difference in their returns, but also leaving it in that account to depreciate rather than investing it in something that could reap bigger rewards in the form of dividends or higher interest due to the share or property price increasing and then selling it.

So recently, when we as a family got the share of the house money, I told my folks about peer to peer lending. This is where normal people can offer their money up to lend to other people or companies, for a return kind of like being a private money lending bank or loan company. In some cases this return can be in the form of equity in the companies lent or in others in the form of interest payments, with some of the others having both of these options. Now don't get me wrong, there is an element of risk due to the nature of it being a loan, yes the company may not pay it back, but the rate of return on the interest payments can be a considerable leap from the high street bank interest rates. **Please n**ote that since I started writing this book back on my honeymoon, Mark Carney and the Bank of England have increased interest rates but peer to peer lending is still higher than what you can get from what you would describe as a 'normal' bank.

Anyway, the peer to peer platform that I like and have invested in is called Funding Circle, their website feels like a bank account and is regulated by the FCA the only downside is that the money isn't protected by the £85,000 insurance that most banks have because you can lose your capital (the original amount you've put in). Yes this adds an element of risk but with a hefty projected 7.4% interest rate compared to my banks 1.3% surely it's worth risking some of your money isn't it? Not even a little? Not my folks, nope they'd rather put their money in an account where they don't even get the full interest rate anymore due to monthly fees as well as their beloved Premium Bonds which to me is absolutely mind numbing (although as I'm writing this Dad has literally just text me to say he's won £175 on his Premium Bonds, typical). It absolutely kills me that they love them so much, although I doubt I'd be saying that if they won a million on them but that's pretty unlikely. I'll discuss my hatred for Premium Bonds later in this book.

So Funding Circle is a prime example of my Mom and Dad 'sticking to what they know' missing out on increased rewards in order to avoid taking a risk. I can't even convince them to put a small amount in per month to 'test the water'. Is this because their endowment mortgage 'risk' didn't pay off? Is it because the latest digital finance initiatives have given them too many choices and instead it's just easier to plonk it in a bank? The digital revolution has snuck up on me and I grew up with computers so I kind of understand, but they use internet banking so I guess there's only a small leap, come on you can do it.

Please don't see this chapter as me advising you to put your money in a peer to peer lending scheme, all I'm saying is research other places to put your money and not just assume that the right/ best place is always a bank.

Mom and Dad think: Their money is safe in the bank, i.e. what they have always done.

Reality: Their money is slowly eroding in banks and other types of investments can be more rewarding if due diligence and research is carried out.

CHAPTER 7 THE BLOODY HOUSE THAT JACK BUILT

The phrase 'ooh ya bastard' and this chapter's title were prolific in my childhood. Every weekend, this is all I would hear my Dad shout while he was doing bits of DIY, gardening or car maintenance, bizarrely while mainly lying down on the floor. Did anyone else's Dad do that? Lie on the floor while doing jobs, not swear as I assume they all do that. As a boy, I often pictured him at work lying down fixing a bakery oven (he was a bakery engineer in case you hadn't work that out), shouting the same swear words. He's still to this day, a practical and strong man, physically stronger than me and 30 years my senior, with sausage fingers and hard skin; you know the type, a bloke's bloke. I could always see that these genes had skipped a generation with me; whereas I was more akin to my Mom, being skinny and small and had worked out that I'd much prefer to be in an office than digging a road in the pissing down of rain or fixing a machine covered in oil. Not that there's anything wrong with doing that but it just wasn't and still isn't for me. Dad if you're reading this, I think you're partly to blame for my lack of manual skills as you did most of this type of work for me and my Mom, which was commendable but may have been a little short sighted. Just this weekend, he was up a ladder fixing my living room 'big light' because I couldn't. Oh the shame of it! Also, it's probably like Teen Wolf where it has actually skipped a generation. Note to self, check to see if Dad is actually a werewolf.

I digress, but you get the picture, anything that needed doing around the house my Dad would undertake himself. A plumber by trade, he'd do tiling, amateur electrics and car maintenance to name but a few, always with a few scrapes on his bald head or bleeding fingers or some other flesh wound. Me and my Mom used to giggle between ourselves when he was swearing. We as a family often quoted the muppets movie 'crazy Harry plays with electrics'. Occasionally, he'd take me outside to see how to check the oil and water on the car but I just wasn't interested and be back inside playing on my Gameboy before he'd got the bonnet open (I'm so unpractical I originally wrote boot instead of bonnet lol). Also, somehow I'd worked out quite early in my life that I could pay someone to do this type of stuff hence even more reason to not needing to pay attention. I do wish I had now but instead I'd sit playing Tetris, safe in the knowledge that my Dad would do any manual tasks or fix the broken things around the house.

Rays 'fixing' was the norm in our house and it was quite good that as a couple they were so industrious and saved money on practical house tasks. I can hardly remember seeing a tradesman in the house who wasn't a friend of my Dad's. I'd come home from school or college and Mom and Dad would both be eager for me to see what they'd achieved and I would dutifully look around to try and notice what 'improvement' they'd made and then they would relish in telling me how little it had cost and how much Dad had hurt himself in the process, this even continued when they lived in France for 8 years, Facetiming me their discounted DIY achievements and injuries to various parts of my Dad's body to my previous girlfriend's horror.

As a child I never questioned it, it was only when I lived in my childhood home when they actually moved to France after retiring that I realised that this DIY may not have been as successful endeavour in the longer term. It was fine at first; their carefully tuned machine of a house that I was temporarily looking after was as I'd always remembered, warm, homely and spacious. It was only when I came to start working on the house, cleaning and decorating I realised that my Dad (encouraged by Mom) was, well, a bit of a bodger. What I mean by this is they'd identify something they'd like to improve usually based on some DIY programme (Changing Rooms etc) and then find the cheapest way of achieving the same effect. Fine you'd think, but the downstream consequences of these actions meant that to do anything new to the house I had to repair other areas/ rooms in order to right the wrongs of their 'improvements' over the previous 28 years to just make a start on a new job. And with me not being practical, you can imagine, it meant that I was at the mercy of tradesmen. And because the house still technically belonged to my parents I would run decisions and check prices with them, which would inevitably lead them to state that I was overpaying and my Mom informing me that 'your Dad could do that for nothing when we come over' on Skype calls, 'I know Mom, but that's what caused the problem in the first place!'.

Oh what a predicament. A lovely 3 bedroom house with awful tiles on top of awful old tiles in the kitchen, horrible artex that they wanted removed that they just painted over and over until it looked like a flake chocolate bar because they wouldn't pay a plasterer to skim it or overboard it, solid wood floor finished off with doweling, hopefully you get the idea. So basically I just couldn't start any jobs on the house without it costing me a small fortune righting the wrongs that had been done over their reign of terror. So being a lazy git, guess what? I didn't. Yes that's right I didn't do anything (except the bathroom but even then my lack of practical skills shone through by taking a sledgehammer to the ceiling and exposing the loft!). I am a lazy impractical bastard; Frank Spencer meets Garfield, if you will!

My parent's desire to save money and not use trades people had a few other negative effects over and above my Dad's surface injuries and my premature understanding of the word 'bastard'. Firstly, the poor quality finish of the house meant that when we came to sell it we had to accept at below market value as anyone with a pinch of common sense could see how much work there was to do to put it right. Secondly, the time spent by my Dad could have been put to other more constructive uses, money earning and/ or relaxing. Lastly, they could have enjoyed the house more as it would have had a more quality finish but just to slightly argue with myself (as I often do) this may have been and probably was their idea of fun and lovely time spent together albeit seemingly stressful and costly to me and the outside world.

I'm not saying that there's anything wrong with DIY far from it, the small bits that I have done throughout my life have given me a sense of pride and achievement but I have also experienced a sense of pride when I've paid for tradesmen to come in and do some work and experiencing their excellent results or relief that they were injured, knackered or both rather than me. My parents were shocked to hear how much I'd paid for certain things like the bedroom decorating on my new 'old' house but after their initial reaction even they appreciated the quality of the job. I also appreciated the time saved by not having to do the work myself and the lack of chance of hurting myself physically or my pride when faced with difficulty in the process. The lovely wife, Mrs Jones likes doing stuff, partly to save money and partly to get the sense of achievement, so we've come to an agreement that anything more than painting the house or mowing the lawn gets done by a professional, or her brother in-law who's a pretty handy chap too. Also, it's probably worth noting that the use of tradespeople is less risky nowadays compared to the bad old days when my Mom and Dad would be trying to get work done. This is thanks to clever internet things such as checkatrade.com etc and asking for recommendations on Facebook. I guess the chance to have a bad review has marginalised the bodgers and the 'no shows' leaving the quality workers to stay in the game and the rest to piss off.

Mom and Dad think: Do everything around the house yourself because it's 'cheaper' than paying a trades person.

Reality: If you do everything yourself, you can waste time, money and energy for poorer results. Also, there are unseen side effects such as self-inflicted injuries and expensive damage that may cost you more to correct your property further down the line.

CHAPTER 8
CHEAP MECHANIC

As mentioned earlier in the book my Dad loves to save money and hates paying someone for something he thinks he could do himself for cheaper and/or for free. In some instances this is totally true and he kept our old boiler going for 29 years. I mean he was a plumber by trade but surely from a safety perspective this was wrong? I'm not going to mention the fact that the energy efficiency of a newer boiler alone would have saved them a fortune far outstripping the cost of a new boiler plus installation, but hey ho it's done now.

Anyway one thing my Dad liked to do if he couldn't do something himself was get someone else who he knew to do it for him. This meant he could a) get it done cheaper than a paid professional that he didn't know and b) have a lovely chat with the person fixing it while getting it done (I inherited my chattiness from him!). And for car repairs he had a friend who would fix cars for cheap and even though he's a lovely guy, let's just say the repairs weren't exactly always the best quality and you definitely got what you paid for. Recently this was mentioned by my best man at my wedding (I started this on my honeymoon remember?), as his Dad did used this friend lots too. It must have been a Tipton 'Dad' thing to do.

So this was the car repair man and to be fair to him, he saved us a few quid in car repairs over the years, especially when I had an old mini for my first car! One of the repairs that still makes me chuckle was some black tape that covered some rust on my best mate's Dad's wing mirror. Lol. I'm not questioning the guy's work he is what he is, a backstreet garage but what I am questioning is my Dad's unquestioning loyalty/ frugality of using him and how far my Dad would go out of his way in order to use him. Ok, if you're within a 50 mile radius yes I agree, why not go to someone you know that you can have a chat with and won't charge you the earth for something, that's fine. However, my Dad started to go to ridiculous lengths to use this garage for MOTs and general repairs. I didn't work it out at first, but when they moved to France for eight years, there seemed to be a pattern of their visits back to me. It was round about Dad's MOT renewal, where he'd be just 'popping round' to the mechanic's to say 'hello'. To my surprise (and slight miffed offness) I worked out that they were timing their visits to coincide to what needed to be done to the car. I mean WTAF?! He wouldn't have his car fixed locally in France but drive himself and my Mom (in the car that needed repairing or checking) hundreds of miles across to another country and over the channel back to use his mate to do the work! Jesus, ok he wouldn't charge for a wiper blade but how much fuel/danger/effort to get this free wiper blade? What a ridiculous state of affairs?

Even when we first moved to our new house and they moved to Wales, he did try and stay at ours as the mechanics is closer to ours than theirs, in order to make a visit but my Mom finally put her foot down by shouting his full name and told him that he wasn't allowed to use family visits as an excuse for getting his car done anymore even though he still pops in to see the mechanic on the way back to Wales every now and then.

Update 1: He has since found a Welsh equivalent near to where they live and we all have a good laugh about his loyalty to a cheap mechanic. I have contemplated that if he moves somewhere else whether or not he'll have the same loyalty to the Welsh equivalent?

Update 2: I've recently had an MOT done and rather than using the main dealer I think I may have found my equivalent of my Dad's cheap mechanic near to where I live. Like father like son ay?

Update 3: My Mom turned 65 yesterday and interviewed her for my podcast, called 'The World According to AJ1' and when questioned about how she felt about being in this book, this chapter was the only one she mentioned.

Mom and Dad think: Use a cheap mechanic that you know will save you money.

Reality: The continuous scrimping can cost you money in the short term and almost definitely will in the long run.

Mom and Dad think: It's worth travelling miles to a cheap mechanic

Reality: The amount of fuel and ferry tickets and time spent is really not worth the saving on a wiper blade. Plus your kid might feel a bit used if you only visit to get your car fixed!

CHAPTER 9
CHARITY BEGINS
AT HOME

First of all, just to let you know I had planned to write this chapter today anyway and bizarrely, Rob Moore has just done a live feed on Facebook on the very same subject. It must be fate!

How many of your parent's state 'charity begins at home' though I've not heard my folks state this but I've heard lots of people from their generation say it. My Mom and Dad are very generous people, if we visit they don't let us lift a finger (to the point of frustration for Claire as she likes to be busy) and they also buy in lots of our favourite things to make us feel welcome when we stay, they live quite far away so this is a must. They give lovely gifts for Christmas and birthdays, even though some of the gifts for Finley have been slightly premature like a giant 'animal' from the muppets t-shirt when he was first born lol. But they are definitely not tight.

However, when it comes to giving to charity apart from the odd homeless man and my Mom working for Barnardo's back in the day they don't really give much to anyone outside the family. I remember them actively, switching off Comic Relief when it was on the TV (although come to think of it I'm not sure my Dad was that keen on Lenny Henry!). For me this was normal and frankly it's none of my business what they do with their money or how much they give away (says the man writing a book about it!). I never challenge them on this as it's their money that they can do with what they like with. But it just seems a little odd that they are so generous in some ways but rarely donate to charities unless it's giving Finley money to put in the charity box or the postcode lottery which I don't really see as giving to charity, just another chance to win some money. *Correction: while proof reading this my Mom has informed me that they give to the Welsh Air Ambulance every month, so that's told me hasn't it?

Now in the majority of books that I have read, it states that to be truly rich you need to give some of your money away and definitely not hoard it. The mind-set is that the more you give the more the universe gives back I don't know how much I think the 'universe' gives it back but I do kind of think that Karma is a thing and truly believe you can attract positivity by giving out positivity and if you give out you probably will get something back at some point. The Noel Gallagher and Ian Brown song lyrics; 'keep what you got by giving it all away' says it beautifully. From the books I've read, Rich Dad Poor Dad's Rich Dad (yes I did mean to write that) proclaimed that if he needed more money he would give tithing (a donation) to the church, this he believed, in turn would return in the form of one of his stocks doing well or a business deal or a sum of money. I decided to take this on board after all this was a book written by a rich person and I wanted to be like them. What did I have to lose? I can afford some charity donations can't I? I can now I think and tell myself I can! I decided to give 10% of my wages and I have to admit it's easier said than done.

As mentioned, I've grown up with my parents being generous to me as well as friends, family and the occasional homeless man or woman so at first I found it quite natural to give to more homeless people and charities but only really in moderation, a quid here or there. This was partly because I've perceived myself to be broke, I wasn't actually broke, and I just thought I was (and as discussed I was creating scarcity with this mind set). I didn't have much empathy because I've not really owned anyone else's problems enough to feel the need to donate any more. The perceived loss of the money had reduced the desire to donate generously to a cause other than myself just in case I needed it. Is this you? Do you proclaim to be broke when asked on a night out? Is that really your reality? Or do you say to homeless, I haven't got any change to spare? Just think if the universe is listening, you're screwed!

Giving away 10% of my wages was and still is harder than I first thought, yes what a 'first world problem' poor me! For instance, it's hard to know who to give the money to, I started with a few charities I'd supported before, but soon got bored of giving to the same ones with the same thank you messages and having worked for and alongside charities I know a lot of my donation could go towards wages of the people working for them and not always reaching the person it was originally intended for, so the inner cynic in me needed more. I didn't realise this was a factor until I started writing this chapter but that thought does enter my mind when I see the adverts on TV for a big charity, I do wonder whether the small African child gets to see any of what is donated and lament at the fact that the charity had to pay a production company or in house film bod to produce the very advert to get the cash. This is quite deep but probably for my podcast and not this book!

I wanted to start giving to more tangible, more real 'worthy' causes. So I started trawling Facebook for friends who had recommended charities or set up Justgiving pages for a sponsored run or similar. I have to admit that this was a little bit of fun too as in a Brewster's Millions style attempt to spend the 10% I made large donations to friends and family's sponsorship pages. Sometimes anonymously, sometimes with my face, sometimes I just wrote it on the sponsor sheet at the tea point at work. All of the receivers seemed to be shocked and grateful by my 'generosity'. Sometimes I was approached by people that weren't being sponsored to tell me how generous I was. I even got an email from Justgiving.com stating I was in the top 1% of people donating for a month; this baffled me as I was still within my 10% of my wages so how could I be the top 1% when there are so many people regularly giving to charity?

If I'm honest it had started to become a little bit of an addiction (told you I had an addictive personality) and soon realised this had become way more about me and my vanity than the charity or the person being sponsored which in itself I knew was wrong. This realisation came when a close friend of mine at work refused to accept a large donation to a chosen charity for someone's leaving when I wasn't even that close to the person leaving. I came back down to earth with a bump and subsequently went back to anonymising my donations or only donating generously to people I'm very close to. Anyway, this activity had made me realise that it's really good for the soul to give and have since started to make random anonymous donations to causes that are not as well supported on Justgiving. In following this course of action I found that well supported charities albeit localised personal ones have an element of momentum and I feel that my money is better given to the underdog rather than the big ones in order to get their momentum going. It also feels better being anonymous as my ego is taken out of it. I also try not to tell anyone I've done it unless I'm raising awareness for the charity itself with a view of getting other people to donate.

Also, reading Rich Dad Poor Dad and Money by Rob Moore has taught me that to bring wealth into your life you need to give and increase the energy/ flow about money perhaps even giving to people that aren't necessarily destitute like giving a big tip to a waiter or waitress or paying for someone else's lunch etc. So I decided to try this for myself (I even quizzed Rob Moore on how to get the nerve to do this while he was doing a 'ask me anything' Facebook Live video). I have to admit, when I started to give away time and cash more often, a few unusual things started to happen. Firstly, it's quite hard to do to begin with, lots of things go through your mind, will the person receiving the donation judge me for being too generous, will I get mugged, will people think I'm being snooty and looking down my nose at them? I realised that this is a muscle you have to work on and I did, forcing myself to give to strangers, homeless and paying for random things for people. It gets easier with time but I do have mixed emotions at the point of giving as well as judging myself or the person/ organisation/ group that I was giving to. Are they grateful enough? Are they too grateful? Do they act nicely towards me now because I've given not because they are nice or they do actually like me? All of these are questions that I've had to work to quash in my mind.

So what have I found from this philanthropy? Magically, rather than being broke and having less money because of giving it away, I have found that I am better off when I give. Bizarrely, money and opportunities to make money have started to appear usually shortly after a donation of some kind. Not instantly, like I gave a pound to someone and I get a pound off someone else but things like business opportunities, money gifts and other ideas appeared once I had been kind in some way. They were like mini delayed gifts; almost as if the act of giving had opened me up to receiving. I also got positive feelings like that good things were coming to me and bizarrely, when I gave a lot I felt wealthy too. You should try it, you might like it.

The other side effects were good too, it felt good to give, I did it mainly anonymously and knowing that I'd helped someone gave me a warm fuzzy feeling and my friend and former colleague Mo Abdel-Gadir co-creator of Gratitude Lifestyle informed me that our brains release the same pleasurable endorphins for giving as are released from receiving. Take your mind out the gutter and think about that for a second, we experience the same pleasure from giving that we do from receiving. So all of these times you're asked to give, you could be getting some little positive experience but by saying 'no', you've blocked that opportunity of a little more positivity in your life. I recommend reading Yes Man by Danny Wallace, it's not only funny but has a strong message of whereby saying 'yes' to things rather than 'no' he bought more good things into his life. Rather than 'I don't have any change' giving the guy a quid, you might get thanks or a 'bless ya', you might not get anything from him but you can guarantee a little thanks to yourself for acknowledging that you do have change and you're lucky to have the job that you can afford to spare a quid to do this.

This positive phenomenon is probably why shopping is pleasurable, maybe because you 'give' the shop assistant the sale and hand over the money. It's just that due to fair trade (the tradition not the brand) we have come to expect something in return for giving. Maybe this is why my folks give to the postcode lottery as it's for charity but they 'get' a chance to win something. I must stress at this point my parents do give some but a lot of the older generations I have encountered are more reluctant to give. Think of the rich people in show business or even in the world and how much they give to charity; Robbie Williams, Bill and Melinda Gates etc they do not seem to be worried about giving money away and it doesn't seem to affect them financially either. They aren't worried about it not coming back and bankrupting themselves are they? Maybe just maybe they've worked out that if they give it out it comes back to them.

Previously, the cynic in me wondered if there are

tax incentives for giving to charity but maybe that was my parent's cynicism coming out in me. Maybe there are maybe there aren't why should it bother me is probably the question I should be asking myself? The other question I had was, is it a chicken and egg effect, in other words do the richer people give because they are rich or do they become rich because they give? Obviously, if you have more 'disposable income' you wouldn't begrudge a man a quid on the street but if you only have a fiver in your bank account to last you a week you may be more reluctant to give or at least wish to get some reassurances of what he's going to be spending it on before you donate. It would take even more persuading if you had people reliant on you; children and elderly parents etc. What if you knew that pound coin would bring £2 back in some other form, then it would be a no brainer; maybe those that give have more faith and what is known as abundance mentality. There's more coming so don't sweat it, maybe those without this trait struggle to attract money because they miss this belief and thus generate scarcity for themselves because that's all they can perceive.

I don't think anyone is saying give all your wages away as that would be silly and pointless to go to work for. If you take a genuine look at your finances you should be able to give small amounts here and there. It won't harm you or skint you out and the pleasure of doing so is worth it and you might just help someone in the process to live another day or help to feed their family. I remember a friend saying to me don't give to homeless people because they might buy drink or drugs with it, I said to them if I was living on the streets that's what I'd buy so why should I judge them? We laughed and walked on but the conversation stayed with both of us, maybe because we had the privilege to walk on and laugh about it whereas the poor men and women on the streets don't have that luxury.

Mom and Dad think: Charity begins at home.

Reality: The more you give the better you feel. The better you feel the more positive things come your way thanks to the law of attraction.

CHAPTER 10
LEVERAGE

As mentioned earlier, in 2015 my friend and occasional business partner lent me his copy of the Cash Flow Quadrant by Robert Kyosaki to me, and wow, it was like someone had unplugged me from the matrix and introduced me to another world that was there in front of me all along but I couldn't see it. From there I went on to read lots more of these books and the most influential author in this field for me was Rob Moore and his books; Money and Life Leverage. They taught me that if I wasn't leveraging then I was probably being leveraged. What did they mean by this? Essentially, that in life there are those people that are doing things for others and those that are being done for, most of us are usually a mixture of both but some people can be at either end of the spectrum. For instance, me and my wife leverage each other, because she likes to clean and I like to cook we leverage each other to do the things we like rather than the things we don't like to do. I guess this is a good example of a partnership too.

If you have a full time job rather than being unemployed or self-employed your company is leveraging your skill whatever that may be by offering you a sum of money per hour that you undertake that skill for them. It's like this is a detail missed from lessons at school and money advice on the TV.

But what we're ignoring is that our jobs take up so much of your bloody life up that you don't get time to spend the money you earn or have the opportunity to earn any more money and/ or leverage someone or something else. Before reading the Money Guru books, I'd run little businesses so I'm sure there was an entrepreneur somewhere hiding in me before I'd read them but the thing I'd missed or not been shown was the other key message which is the power of leverage; the use of something to its maximum advantage or in financial terms borrowing something (time/ money/ assets) to earn more money from it which equalled more than the sum being leverage. The primary mistake in my entrepreneurial endeavours was that I was doing everything myself, leaving me no free time to do other more profitable activities. What I forgot to do was outsource and leverage someone else's time, so I was always going to be a busy fool. Obvious, when I now step back and look at it.

I thought I was being savvy but actually using my time that I could be earning more money elsewhere on lower value tasks was a mistake. On reading these books I had lots of Homer Simpson 'doh' when

I realised where I'd been going wrong and also the thought about everyone else in my life doing the same as I was and realising about those leveraging me to do things for them.

Anyway, I've tried explaining these concepts to my Mom and Dad and others of their generation and they're not having any of it. It's like they don't want to be unplugged from the matrix and that's their choice but I find it very frustrating, as my parents are so forward thinking about so many things except for property, money and investing.

This book is meant to be part of my way to unplug them but I'm not sure if it's going to work. Think about their approach to DIY, they're totally unleveraged because they do it all themselves. I am currently typing this while a guy called Dave is plastering my staircase, so I'm leveraging his time and skill so I can do this which should generate money for me more than the cost of him doing it and definitely less chance of a bodge job!

I wish Mom and Dad would just think about it, if you buy a car for £10k, you use it, it depreciates and you end up selling it for less than you paid for it after insuring and maintaining it for years, unless you're a taxi driver and leveraged it. All it has done is taken you to and from work. If you buy a house with the same £10k and leverage the bank for a mortgage for another £50k, you now have your name on an asset that will probably go up in value over time (you only lose when you sell!), you then stick some tenants in there for £400 per month and you're leveraging their money to pay the mortgage for the property that you own and use the cash flow to pay for a lease car. All with the same £10k, it's that simple. So how do I communicate this to my parents? I think I'm just going to have to do it for myself and then show them my bank balance with the cash flow coming in, surely they can't argue with that evidence? Actually, my Dad probably could.

Update: I am currently reading a book called No Money Down Property Investing and this is even better than purchasing the asset with your own money as basically, you don't need to get mortgages, you can do things called 'rent to rent' and 'letting options'. Check it out as it's even further out of the matrix than I was before. Just need to grow the balls to do it now.

Mom and Dad think: Get one job working for a company and then keep the money that you earn safe in a bank.

Reality: You need to use your income to buy assets to sustain long term cash flow from multiple streams of income as well as leveraging other people's time and money through mortgages and delegation.

CHAPTER 11 GODDAM PREMIUM BONDS

Oh my life, Premium Bonds must have had the best marketing strategy ever back in the day as everyone over the age of 60 seems to bloody love em. Even with their money god Martin Lewis denouncing them they still plough their hard earned cash into them. If my Dad mentions Ernie to me once more I'm gonna shuv his kindle up his ass. Ok AJ1 you've been going on about these things all through this book, what's your beef? Well for starters it's not a savings account; they don't guarantee any returns on your money, they only guarantee you'll get the same figure that you put in so not working or earning for you. You don't lose anything but then again I don't 'lose' anything if I just buried it in the back garden, ok well I might lose some if the neighbours saw me do it and steal it, but you get my point. Also if you remember the earlier chapter about inflation by only guaranteeing to receive your principal (the money you started with) back, if you don't win, which is quite likely given the odds calculator on Martin's website, then you've actually lost money overall!

It's like some weird OAP gambling cult. You put your money in, they run a draw and you might get £10 up to £1 million, notice the word 'might', you might also get sod all. So they're a bit like the pools or the lottery except you get your original bet back, all the time this money is doing some other shit for other people while you're hanging about for a 'winner' to pop out. I mean just the randomness! Your money is being leveraged people, wake up and smell the coffee!

Anyway, I truly believe that this is seen as 'investing' to my parents. But will they listen to me when I tell them it's not prudent to put their money in there? Nope they're still believing what they've been taught, like my wife not understanding that you shouldn't wash fresh chicken, it's what she's been taught to do and difficult to break the habit or remove the learned behaviour to my increased frustration. Why am I such an angry man?! Incidentally there's a massive sticker on chicken nowadays saying 'do not wash fresh chicken' wonder if I could put a sticker 'these are crap' on the Premium Bonds website in the same way? Doubt it, my hacking days stopped at piracy of Amiga 600 games in 1995, for the younger ones amongst you think of a more modern reference like jailbreaking your Iphone.

Update: just spoken to my Dad and he's had £50 from £50,000 and they think it's good.

Just think of the opportunities they are missing out on with their money in Premium Bonds, they could have a couple of mortgages with a couple of tenants in, they could have it in blue chip shares, any f*cking thing, but no. My business studies teacher eloquently described this as 'opportunity cost', by putting money in one place you are relinquishing the opportunity to put it somewhere else that is more profitable. Smart money moves it to higher yielding investments; my folks put it into Premium Bonds.

I can't say any more on this, Premium Bonds, just NO!

Mom and Dad think: Premium Bonds are the dog's bollocks.

Reality: Premium Bonds are actually just bollocks. It's just structured gambling with your money back. Come on people!

CHAPTER 12
YOUR SHARES
ARE DOING WELL

This is the most confusing chapter of the whole book for me. When my Dad retired but before my Mom did the same he spent a lot of time at home, cooking lovely food like pakoras and curries, but mainly when me and my girlfriend at the time got home from work or university he would be lying down either in the sun or on the sofa. And if he was on the sofa, the TV would be on, invariably would be what me and my Mom called 'scrolling tele' so stuff like Bloomberg or NBC; the scrolling being the share price tickers and news headlines along the bottom and side of the screen. He'd talk to me at length about the share prices and impacts of different news stories on future share prices, I have to be honest sometimes I was interested and sometimes I wasn't. Looking back it was great insight, most of which, in time has come true. So this then begs the question, why didn't he invest himself? He has no shares to his name. If he had such a good understanding of the stock market and currencies in line with what was happening politically I just don't get why he didn't stick a cheeky few hundred in. Why didn't he put his money where his mouth was? And why so interested in something he had no skin in the game of? He was probably biding his time for a big Premium Bonds win. Lol. I'll phone him and ask him tomorrow.

I phoned him and it turns out that he was interested to see where his pension was heading. His pension scheme included Allied foods and Primark to name a couple and he liked to see what was happening. He always thanks Claire for buying clothes from Primark as it contributes to his pension pot, and I suppose this answers my question partly. I do however, feel that there's something missing from this story, maybe he had a dabble and lost big and just doesn't talk about it, maybe it comes back to the feeling of scarcity, the greater desire to provide for his family than risk it on stocks and shares in what he would see as a gamble, or maybe technology such as stock dealership apps has made it easier to invest for my generation.

Even now, whenever I see him or speak on the phone we always have a chat about how my shares have been doing. Yes, despite my Dad's aversion to the stock market, I dipped my toe a few years ago and then started seriously investing once I got some National Grid shares at a discounted price from where

I work which is a former subsidiary of National Grid. He keeps an eye on the ones in my portfolio but never invests himself. Weird!

I guess living through financial crashes would have this effect. He's a clever person and has a Kindle Fire with the internet on it, so in today's age could easily make a small investment but chooses to follow my portfolio rather than take the risk on himself. I understand that investing is not for everyone but I really don't understand his interest if that is the case. One day maybe I'll found out that Gordon Gecko was based on him and he lost big and went to prison. Maybe I've had too many diet cokes for one day and need to go to bed. Good night.

Mom and Dad think: Shares are too risky.

Reality: Everything is risky including money in the bank.

CHAPTER 13
I'LL HAVE A SWIMMING POOL PLEASE

This was my Mom's standard phrase right from the day I got my degree, then my first job and then any subsequent promotions and still is to this day if anything positive happens with money. She also said it to my 5 year old son Finley the other day when he told her he was going to be an artist. The woman wants a goddam swimming pool, we get it! And I hope that one day I'll be able to provide that for her. The only problem with this desire is that standard, albeit well paid jobs are not the answer to getting a swimming pool even though it would seem logical from the generation that she's from. This advocated work + high wages = bigger house with swimming pool, right? Wrong!

My Mom and Dad were so cool during my GCSE's

and subsequent education their attitude towards me was always 'do your best, and we'll love you no matter what the outcome'. They gently pushed me to revise but never forced me to, if I didn't want to go to school I didn't have to which made me want to go, bizarrely. But the underlying tone of their approach was don't worry, just get what you can and we'll help you get a job, no expectations although I do remember my Mom did like the idea of me being a lawyer when I came home and proclaimed that was what I wanted to be one albeit very briefly after reading about a Legal Executive job at a careers fayre. I even did A Level Law and scraped a C grade, though her dream of me being a lawyer came to an end when it dawned upon me that I had to do a lot of reading to become one. I bet she still wishes that I'd gone in to being one, the Hyacinth Bucket part of her.

I am currently well paid, I have been for a considerable amount of time now, however, the house with the swimming pool hasn't manifested yet. You've probably guessed where this is going, but it is unlikely that being well paid will get me to the point of slapping a big fat cheque down and handing my Mom her swimming costume. I hope that you've gleaned from this book so far that you need to utilise your income and make the most of it by leveraging and making money from your original sum (the principal) and not just hoard/ save it in the bank as they had prescribed to me. You need to get to the point where you can replace your job wages with your passive income by taking advantage of leverage and compounding.

Mark Homer promotes the use of compounding in his book Uncommon Sense, this means the more you get the more you earn and then plough that back in to earn money as well on top of that. He advocates putting your money into places (accounts) that earn compound interest because over time the money that you're earning from your principal is then added to the principal and increases the money that will be accumulating the interest on leading to a large constantly growing pot. The longer you can do this without removing any of the principal or the interest the better off you will be fact. Couple this with a healthy property portfolio (also using leverage) a half decent stocks and share portfolio as discussed earlier and maybe just maybe you might get a house with a swimming pool and one for your mom too.

There are other downsides to the one job one income approach other than not becoming rich. Firstly, the rewards for the hard work you undertake are capped at a certain amount. What I mean by this is, if you are working for ICI and you invent a way to achieve alchemy (turning lead into gold) and you are on their property using their materials and equipment, ICI own the patent and future rewards of your invention. I know this because I once met one of the inventors of cling film working as a teaching assistant at a college because, yes you've guessed it, he was working for ICI when he invented it so didn't get any riches from doing so. What a pisser for him?! But even if you're not an inventor and you just work in a normal job, no matter how good your place of work is with dishing out rewards for hard work, your income is still a filtered percentage of what the organisation earns and then chooses to give you, could you earn more money doing what you do now but for yourself? Could you do it part time alongside your job supplementing your income until you've got enough clients to walk away from the day job? Just a thought!

Also, the more eggs you put into one basket ironically, is more risky. I bet most of you assume that a permanent position within a successful company is a less risky employment strategy than becoming self-employed or an entrepreneur or both but you might be incorrect in that belief. Think about it, there are so many things that could side swipe your comfortable day job and take you off your current route. The company you work for might hit hard times or even go bankrupt and may have to lay people off. They might relocate leaving you with a travel dichotomy where you have a job but it's too expensive or takes too long to get there. You or a family member might get sick. You may have another or several mouths to feed. You may lose your driving license (particularly poignant if you're a driver). Their might be a new piece of legislation or competitor or technology that might put your company out of business. If any or all of these happened, your current lifestyle would have a large question mark over it. So it makes sense to diversify and at least increase the amount of ways you earn money (in other words multiple income streams) even if it's alongside your day job, protect the downside, get other forms of income, because as Forrest Gump says 'life is like a box of chocolates, and sometimes you get a f*cking chocolate penny eugh!'.

Finally, and maybe more importantly, one of the main positives to working for yourself is that your earnings are limitless, by this I mean you can go out and earn more and more if you choose to or take it easy if you want to. Remember a day job is just what it says it is, a job that takes your day.

Mom and Dad think: One well paid job will make you rich and manifest as a mansion with a swimming pool.

Reality: Your job for a single employer not only makes someone else rich, it is also risky as a change of circumstance could mean that you have to start all over again.

CHAPTER 14 THE DAY THE DEBT COLLECTOR ARRIVED (MY MISTAKE!)

My Dad is a clever guy, sometimes too clever for his own good, like a lot of Dad's can be; I am now I'm a Dad lol and I know I am way too 'clever' for my own good. My Dad is the type of man that if he was your 'phone a friend' on Who Wants to Be a Millionaire TV quiz show, you're not quite sure he would give you the answer that is standard knowledge that would be correct or give you some insider conspiracy theory that he saw on the History Channel or spend so long telling you the origins of the answer that you'd run out of time. I think you get the picture, he knows a lot and he loves to share it, oh and I've also noticed of late, that if he doesn't know the answer to a direct question he will tell you every-thing he knows related to the topic to steer you away from the fact that he doesn't know the answer to the original question that you asked him. I'm on to you Bastard Face!

So what's this got to do with title of the chapter? As I mentioned in an earlier chapter, my Mom and Dad moved to France for a while, shortly after they had both retired. On doing so, my Dad, whom still had some credit card debt (tut tut!) and a few bills in this country dutifully went to the bank to sort out all of his direct debits and standing orders in preparation for him not being in the country so he and my Mom could enjoy their retirement in peace. Well the other thing about my dad is that he loves to be centre of attention and tell a good story, and this time he came back and regaled us with a story (in great detail) about the cashiers at the bank and that they were in love with each other and had paid little attention to my Dad's needs during the interaction to which we all laughed. Obviously he wasn't particularly happy about the experience but shrugged it off and we thought nothing more of it.

Shortly after this event they went off to France and I moved into their house as I'd just been through a break up and needed somewhere to live and as they hadn't been able to sell their house. Remember they couldn't sell the house due to all of the bodging mentioned in the earlier chapter. Even though the circumstances weren't ideal it was a win win situation for both of us, as I was giving them rent that was equivalent to a small flat but having the luxury of living in a 3 bed detached house (formerly my childhood home and the house that Jack built!) and they were happy that they didn't have to sell the family home and that they could supposedly trust their tenant and be helpful to their son at the same time. Little did we know that this decision would lead to a situation that could have left us all in the shit?

Soon after they'd gone, as expected their post started to arrive, a few bills here and there, the odd eye examination appointment etc., all seemingly normal letters which I filed in a big bowl on a shelving unit, ready for either posting in one big lot to them or take them across when I visited. And this is where I dropped the proverbial bollock, I was trying not to be nosey into their business (and I was being lazy!) and so I didn't open a single letter unless otherwise instructed by my Dad perhaps if he wanted to see if he had received a particular piece of mail of which he knew what the envelope would look like so I could find it out of the pile of post in the bowl.

As it happened I had a few turbulent life events take place at the time and it took me a while to go and visit them after my first visit when they first moved there. The post kept coming and I kept piling it into the ever increasing 'post dish'. Then one morning there was a loud knock at the door, it was a debt collector asking for the outstanding overdue balance of one of my Dad's credit cards. I understandably shit my pants and quickly phoned them to ask what the hell was going on, they'd gone to France with a retirement lump sum in their back pocket and I was paying them rent so why the call from the heavy squad? Were they in some kind of trouble they'd never let me in on? Were they always broke and had spiralling debt? Had they absconded to France to avoid their creditors gangster stylee? I was bemused and so were they.

You'll never guess what? Dad was only correct about the bank people paying more attention to each other than what they were doing for him, and had put his direct debits and standing orders exactly one day late every month so his account was receiving a charge that was not being paid off or resolved every month on one of his accounts and as my Dad did not have an e-mail address (discussed later in this book!), they were sending demanding red letters to me and I was dutifully filing them in a dish. What a tit? This only came to light while I opened the entire 'post dish' on an extremely fraught Skype call to my folks. My Dad spoke to the bank and paid off what he needed to but for a short period after that I opened every little bit of mail and had a small poo in my pants whenever there was a knock at the door.

So what's the moral of this chapter? No one was really at fault and the circumstances are pretty random and statistically quite unlikely to happen to you but I guess it's probably worth reminding you that banks (and their computers) are run by people that are fallible and might even be in love with each other. Don't just trust that by asking for something to be undertaken that it will definitely be done or indeed done correctly, always check. Be sure to open your communications from your bank and just double check your accounts that what you think is happening, actually is happening. Otherwise you might be receiving a knock on the door and the need for a new set of under crackers.

Mom and Dad think: We can trust our son and the bank with our property and affairs.

Reality: Could they f*ck!?

CHAPTER 15
NO EMAIL

As discussed in the previous chapter, up until recently my Dad has been proud of the fact that he hasn't had a computer but more importantly an email address or any access to email. In a way I admired this for some time, like a warrior making a stand against the onslaught of technology and the future, but looking back, in particular to the circumstances surrounding the last chapter. I think his stubbornness towards progress has hindered his financial situation or at least not made it any better.

When he is telling us a story about complaining to a bank or energy company for them making a mistake, he used to proudly say the phrase 'they said to me we sent you an email, and I said 'you haven't cause I haven't got one' and in his mind he's the hero and to the person at the other end of the telephone is probably rolling their eyes and doing a wanker gesture to their mate next to them. I would! Technology has moved on and he hasn't, like someone only listening to vinyl and refusing to listen to

MP3s because they're proving some kind of musical purest point. Come on Dad! You're better than this, and bizarrely, he is probably the person that would most benefit from email and electronic banking as his last two homes have been in the countryside cut off from the world. Also, he used to be first to have everything, I remember him sitting programming a union jack into our spectrum 128k for a whole weekend only to discover he'd missed a speech mark or something out of the text and he had to go all the way back through the programme to eventually get it to work. Good times! To be fair I'm the same with Fin now I want to do something remarkable or exciting every time I see him, so stay up all night carving a minion pumpkin or some shit like that.

A few years ago we bought my Dad a Kindle, which forced him to have an email address. I must say now he has it, it feels like he is going through the evolution of email like when email first came about and chain letters and gifs were abundant, instead of these things he sends me articles from the Daily Mail, grr! And also things about my shares in an oil and gas company and Brewdog, yet I can confirm he still hasn't invested himself. Arghhhh why not?!

Anyway, the point of this chapter is to encourage you and your parents to not be too afraid of new technology, in particular in the banking arena. The stuffy banks full of queues at lunchtimes have been replaced by our mobile phones in the form of apps.

Banks are evolving; you need to evolve with them to avoid being left behind or in a situation similar to the debt collector one we were in. Martin Lewis is a good resource to find out how to do these things safely.

Dad thinks: It's cool not to have an e-mail address

Reality: So not cool, move with the times or it could bite you on the ass.

CHAPTER 16
SEE A PENNY
PICK IT UP

When I was at school a guy called Steven Jarvis (nice chap from what I can remember) was bought up in front of the rest of the school at assembly for a positive reason which was unusual at the rough school that I went to. He was asked to appear because he'd managed to find about £50 in loose change he'd found on the floor of the playground at our school (over a period of time not in one day!). This was pretty impactful for the rest of us as £50 at the age of 13 would be like being a millionaire as an adult. The reason; pennies and two pence's from our change were thrown or dropped on the floor, was because we perceived them to have no value. Yet Steven was showing us that by combining all of this change together and then changed at a local corner shop, he now had more cash than the rest of us could dream of at the time. One of the good phrases my Mom and Dad used to say to me was look after the pennies and the pounds will look after themselves and Steven had demonstrated this perfectly.

My Nan used to say to me 'see a penny pick it up, for the rest of the day you'll have good luck' or some clever dick who I can't remember now said to me once 'for the rest of the day you'll have a penny', either way it was meant to be a clever rhyme to get me to pick up money from the floor, but it seems that modern day folk have stopped valuing change like us when we were at school and drop change and definitely wouldn't be seen dead picking it up. Perhaps because we as a society think that it's a bit scruffy to do so. This came to light when I went to London with a friend from work the other week. I saw a coin on the floor and picked it up and with a look of disgust; he said 'what the hell are you doing?' visibly shocked that I would do such a thing. I replied 'I'm putting some extra money in my wallet', I then challenged him and asked him how much savings and at what interest rate he would need to have to earn a penny or whatever the denomination I picked up was and how long would he need to have it in there locked away to achieve it, he started to see my point after a few Moments to ponder.

T Herv Ecker, in his book The Millionaire Mindset, asks why we would turn down free money of any denomination if it's sitting there waiting to be taken and doesn't belong to anyone else. He asks what does this say about us and our attitude to money if we don't. He also suggests that the act of picking it up also has a positive impact in the fact that by accepting the money 'given' by the universe you are also saying you are open to more money in other ways whereas if you ignore it or 'refuse' it by not picking it up, you are saying you do not want or need to attract or accept any more money into your life. Essentially, you are valuing money if you pick it up but rejecting more money if you don't.

I always used to pick up bigger coin denominations; 20ps and 50ps but since reading Millionaire Mindset I pick up any coin I see and say thank you in my mind for it. Yes that's right I now pick up any money I see no matter how battered or dirty it is, I simply pop it in my wallet. Bizarrely, I have found the denominations I've been able to find have increased. Recently, a crisp £20 note lay there for me outside a pub the other week; I had a selfie with it I was so chuffed and grateful for it. Get in! Also, I seem to have developed a kind of sixth sense if there's a coin about but I have to admit I might just be imagining that, whatever. When I get home I put it into my son's money box, leave it in my wallet or use it at the self-service check out at the supermarket, you'd be amazed how much it knocks off your shopping cost before paying with a debit card or a note. This of course leaves more in your bank account to earn interest or invest when the time or the investment is right and this is what is known as compounding (discussed earlier).

Emily, my friend at work looked at me in disgust

when I told her my theory about this, she wouldn't pick up anything less than 50p, but I argued that 50p is fifty pennies grouped together so why not just share that over time? I decided not to argue any more about it as I could see she couldn't be arsed to think about it further and to be fair neither could I, so we gossiped about something else.

Mom and Dad think: Not much about this

Reality: All money even tiny denominations are money that can add to your wealth and help you to attract more money and wealth to you.

CHAPTER 17
NETTE WORTH

To be fair this chapter doesn't have that much to do with my Mom, but how could I resist that for a title in a money book about my parents with a Mom called Annette? This is more about how rich people in general assess their wealth and how rich they are. I'm not sure that most people think about their total value except for maybe how much savings they've got or what they earn per hour or just define themselves by their total amount of debt. They definitely never think about their 'net worth' which is the value of all of their assets (cash, shares, home owned etc.) minus the amount of their liabilities (credit card, loan or any other debts) and to be honest neither did I, until I started reading these books about cash flow.

Me and most of the people who I know or have grown up with seem to have some kind of consumer debt (store card, credit card or car loan). I remember the moment I got my first credit card, a Barclay Card, for a student account I got from the Birmingham Law Courts branch of Barclays while at Uni. Even though I was 22 and 'ahem' intelligent enough to get to university I didn't realise the future pain I was unleashing on to myself and potentially others by taking out this future shackle. The particular branch name did cause a slight comedic moment; the look on my Mom's face when she found a cash machine statement from the Brum Law Courts believing me to do be in some kind of trouble. I wasn't it was just the name of the branch the mini statement was from. My Dad always said that my Mom knew if something was wrong with me instinctively by me doing something as small as changing where I'd took my shoes off and this perceived problem sent her motherly instincts into overdrive. It was all explained very quickly but only accepted after about a thousand reassurances that I hadn't had a summons she finally believed me. Turns out this chapter did have a bit to do with my Mom. Also, as an aside it took her moving to France to stop worrying about me as much. She began a life of long distance worrying.

Anyway, I saw the term 'credit' in the title credit card to mean the bank gives you credit for what you should have in some future day when you've got your degree and hopefully got a job or if I'm being totally honest, I actually thought 'free money'. I instantly started to spend it like it was cash assuming, like many of my fellow undergraduates that once we'd graduated we'd 'walk into a job'. Not even our lecturers predicted the lack of graduate jobs post 9/11. So what happened? I graduated and was unemployed for six months. This time was awful, I lost my sense of time, getting up late, going to bed late, losing self-worth, truly feeling awful about myself, and questioning why I couldn't get a job and sadly whether I wanted to be alive. All of the time I was unemployed I was relying on my Mom and Dad's and friend's generosity as well as the demon credit card to continue the lifestyle I was accustomed to at university. Meanwhile my friends were achieving, as they'd sensibly gone to get jobs and started earning. Obviously, eventually I got a job, but it was too late, the circle of debt had begun and I didn't help myself by getting a girlfriend as frivolous with money as I was, that encouraged me to consolidate my debt (bad) which I'm still paying one of the credit cards off to this day. Pants!

My advice here is that if you can do without using credit cards then do so, don't buy luxury items with them and definitely do not take cash from a cash machine with them as they charge you extra for the privilege. I urge you to work out your net worth which is all of your debt minus all of your assets. This will give you a realistic picture of exactly where you are financially and allow you to plan and work out what you need to do to get out of debt or if you're not in debt how to get richer. If you don't ever look at this figure you'll never know the true extent to the hole that you maybe in and as Rob

Moore states you can only do something about your problem if you know exactly what the problem is. I guess you could say you need to 'know your enemy'.

So why did I call this chapter 'Nette Worth' well because your net worth is what all of the money masters say that they measure rather than how much is in the bank or on their credit card. They claim by measuring your net worth you have more of an idea of what you really own and owe and can use this as a barometer for your success or indeed failure. The calculation is simple, what you own in monetary terms i.e. your assets e.g. property, cash and investments, less what you owe, i.e. your liabilities e.g. loans, credit card debt mortgages etc. This calculation will let you know how well you are doing and more importantly give you an honest view of your finances as it is all too easy to conveniently forget your debt and erase it from your mind and focus on your cash in the bank. Have a go at it. I'm almost certain my folks don't do this and I doubt many other 'normal' folk do but if they did I bet they'd be surprised maybe even shocked but also more aware.

If you or someone you know are in serious credit card or loan debt and feel that you can't do anything about it and it's affecting your mental health then please go to Citizens Advice Bureau or there is a National Debtline and the number is 0808 808 4000. Debt is shit but remember it is always solvable, seek advice and support before it gets too far gone. Remember it's only money and there's no shame in admitting that you've f*cked up!

Mom and Dad think: Not sure about credit cards though personally I used to think they were free money.

Reality: Credit cards are definitely not 'free money' and if handled incorrectly your debt can spiral out of control and affect your wider non-financial life and wellbeing.

Mom and Dad think: Not much about net worth.

Reality: How can you improve your finances if you don't know exactly what you're measuring?

CHAPTER 18
THIS BOOK IS
AN ASSET

I feel that thanks to these books, I have started on a journey that will take me further and further towards financial freedom but even though I've shared most of what I've learnt with them I don't feel my parents believe some of the things I've covered in this book. Most of the lessons are hidden in plain sight for us all to see if we were bothered or encouraged to look. For instance, I now understand that I need to make or purchase assets to earn income from and can't rely on savings and a job alone to get me there. Robert Kyosaki shows in his books the long term recurring value of the creation and purchasing of long term assets is the path to wealth. This book that you are holding in your hands or listening to (hopefully enjoying) is an attempt to create myself an asset that produces passive income. Sorry that I didn't write it just for you and your parents but hopefully you understand and maybe even take inspiration to do similar yourselves. What do I really mean by passive income? Well it's how it sounds, an income that you don't have to do much to achieve after an initial effort, in this case sitting on my laptop every night writing it. Once this book has been written and published hopefully people will purchase it and recommend it and that will cause more purchases and then this cycle continues as long as people continue to be interested in the topic and purchasing the book. From my initial effort upfront now, this book will then exist out in the world ready to be purchased as and when people want to read it which will lead to more income for me.

I never really saw my Dad as an entrepreneur, I think he was more of a social entrepreneur because he had and still has lots of friends that he can rely upon when he needs something doing. If I think back he must have had an entrepreneurial streak that was hidden from me. The reason why I'm thinking this is because he used to turn up with bin bags full of Nike and Adidas shell suits or trainers which I could have my pick of when he came home from work early in the morning (he worked shifts, he wasn't burgling before you ask). I still remember him smelling of bread and bringing a bag of toy guns when I was really young thinking this guy is cool as f*ck or whatever the young version of this would have been. He didn't steal them but if I was wearing anything branded chances were it came from a bin bag rather than a high street store but I didn't care I was wearing Adidas Torsion. Maybe he sold the rest on for a bit of a profit or maybe he just had a dodgy mate. He used to do plumbing foreigners too but I don't think he accepted money most of the time. I think back then friends and family paid each other back in other ways, a favour here or there. It was less about money or maybe it was and I was just too young to see or understand it.

Anyway, regardless, I urge you to use whatever talents that you've got or can learn to create or buy yourself an asset that has lasting potential for continued income. You could buy property to charge rent, write music or books, paint pictures, take photographs, anything that you can do, can be sold, so sell it. This income will then add to your wealth and your net worth and can be invested or earn interest which, as discussed, has a compounding effect on your wealth.

Update: I've recently started a podcast, it's called The World According to AJ1, and this is potentially another asset to earn money from. Watch this space.

Mom and Dad think: You only need one job (or the occasional foreigner) to be financially secure.

Reality: You need assets that can be bought or rented over and over again once created giving you income, cash flow and compounding.

Note. The term foreigner is slang for doing a cash job outside of your day job. They are not importing immigrants or anything dodgy like that!

CHAPTER 19 LOYALTY DOESN'T PAY

What if I were to tell you that most banks, insurance companies and energy providers don't reward loyalty in fact quite the opposite? Would you be surprised? Well my Mom and Dad were, and can hold testament to this seemingly counterintuitive phenomenon. Yes they were pained to find out that rather than keeping the customers they already have happy, they would leave these paying a higher price and instead try to attract new customers with sweet deals. Is this you? When was the last time you switched any of the above. I got this knowledge from Martin Lewis and the reason why it's made this book is because it took my Mom and Dad so long to take this advice on board.

My Mom, bless her, was with Barclays for twenty plus years, she'd opened a bank account on West Bromwich high street when she was a little girl and refused to change as 'she'd always been with Barclays'. She was loyal to them as she had grown up with them as 'her bank'. This was understandable but a very naïve thing to do because as Barclays no longer had to work for her business, guess what, they didn't. The bank manager that gave her original account was probably long retired or maybe even dead now and the bank that she had cherished as a child was now (more of) a ruthless money grabbing bastard out for profit over service. Like a drug dealer that knows that you're hooked, nowadays most banks only give a discount or tempting offer to lure new clients into their business and to be fair even that has a finite amount of benefit to the new customer post say 12 months. For my Mom, it was only when Barclays started advertising their deals on TV that she realised how badly they were treating her, she was even more pissed off when she phoned them up and they told her the deal was only for new customers. 'Disgraceful' she claimed, 'I'm leaving you' she told them on the phone in an attempt to shock them into respecting her long service and but to her surprise, they let her leave without a fight, for shame. The reason being my Mom assumed, wrongly that they existed solely for her to put her money into and not to make a profit. It was eye opening to her and disappointing.

It's the same with the energy companies, how many people have you heard in the past say I'm with British Gas for my gas and I'm with MEB for the electricity. They are staunchly with the traditional view of gas for gas and electricity with the electricity company. I can tell you that if this is you or someone you know that this view is wrong! They are happy for you to think this because they are preying on your ignorance or laziness. Ignorance of the following two facts 1) there is now a competitive market out there and no longer one company for each utility and 2) if you decide to switch you will not have to change anything within your house or garden, the pipes and meters are exactly the same no matter which company you are with. Yes, if you switch to a new utility company that wants to win your business as per the banks above, you can save hundreds of pounds a year and it only takes a few minutes to do so. Yes there is a little bit of leg work using the comparison sites but how else could you save or make hundreds of pounds after say one to two hours on the internet? Don't answer that. So your misplaced loyalty to the company that you've always been with is being exploited by these profit making companies. Wake up people! Today, comparing and switching has never been easier, here are a list of sites that will help you:

www.moneysavingexpert.com
www.comparethemarket.com
www.confused.com
www.gocompare.com

Also, and this is hot off the press, if you need to know who your supplier is, you can find it at the link below:

www.findmysupplier.energy

While I'm on the topic, if you haven't already done so, seriously consider getting a water meter. There's a calculation on Moneysaving Expert that can help you with that. My Mom and Dad told me about this one but I'm not changing the title of the book just for that!

Mom and Dad think: Loyalty is rewarded.

Reality: In the main companies are looking for new business rather than trying to keep their current customers, so newbies get the deals and the oldies get shat on!

Update: I have recently renewed my car insurance and they did reward my loyalty by being the cheapest when I did an online comparison, maybe they've worked out that continued business, is the old adage 'a bird in the hand is worth two in the bush'.

CHAPTER 20 WAIT A BITCOIN

When my parents were giving me the 'inheritance' from the house, apart from being told not to lose it all, my Mom had only one other rule, I wasn't 'allowed' to invest in Bitcoin. How dare she?! Well, I can kind of understand this viewpoint as there'd just been a well-publicised crash with the online cryptocurrency and most news and daytime television articles were showing how risky it was, wheeling anyone who'd lost on it out for all to pity with Phil Schofield and Holly Willoughby. Now I am not saying that Bitcoin, cryptocurrency or block chain stuff is totally safe and you should run out and put all of your lifesavings in it, far from it but I am also of the opinion that there are opportunities in this area if you read enough, smart enough and lucky enough. Similar to shares and currency they are investments that *could* turn you a profit if you are sensible. Remember for every loser there's a winner, that's my inner gambler talking so don't listen to me.

I have invested in some cryptocurrency with my own money (sorry Mom!) the reason being that I feel it will grow in the future, as technology and money evolve so will cryptocurrency and surely it's better to be in at the ground level with a small amount of risk rather than having to play catch up further down the line with more of your hard earned dollar? Don't get me wrong I've not chucked loads in there but I think a little every month will grow nicely and if it doesn't I've not lost loads. Remember with all investments, only put in what you can afford to lose and I mean lose completely. It's like anything new, remember one day long ago coins were being introduced rather than a barter system, covered in mud and cow shit some Mom was saying to her son, don't get investing in any of them coins. Someone has to take a risk why shouldn't it be you? I only wish I had this viewpoint earlier. It's like how contactless payments were feared and not adopted straight away, I remember seeing an old lady in a supermarket refusing to use it through fear of fraud but ironically was reading her pin number written in biro taped to her mobile phone. I mean wtf? Lol.

Anyway, I repeat I'm not advising you to invest your life savings I'm just saying investigate what it's all about and if you can understand it and afford to invest a little then do so. If it comes to nothing then it comes to nothing but remember in 'normal' savings accounts inflation and low interest rates are killing your nest egg anyway.

Mom and Dad think: Bitcoin and cryptocurrency is too risky

Reality: Life is risky; research new investment types and take calculated risks to improve your chances of increasing your fortune. Only risk what you can afford to lose though.

Update: My view on cryptocurrency has recently become more sceptical, mainly because they keep inventing new ones which is devaluing them. For now, I will keep what I have and see if it becomes more regulated.

CHAPTER 21
PASSING IT ON

I've already mentioned that I have a little son Finley (by the way he's just turned six since writing this book damn you passage of time!) and I'm not ashamed to admit that I want him to have the best life ever and I intend for him to have all of this extra knowledge that I have learnt by the time that he grows up as well as any future children Claire and I may have while we are able to. She's pregnant at the time of writing this, nearly one year on from the honeymoon. Go us! I want them to have a head start similar to what my parents gave me by working hard and buying their house. Moreover, I want to pass on (the right) knowledge as well as a healthy bank balance. My aim is to give Finley and little tbc most of the advice in this book albeit in a fun way so that when they're older its second nature to not only save money but be able to invest themselves and be prosperous. Kind of like the rhymes that old guy gave is granddaughter in the Davinci Code so she'd know how to access all the dark secret shit lol.

So how am I planning to do this? Well, it's not easy especially as I'm trying to do it subtly, he doesn't live with me all of the time and his Mom and step Dad where he lives have their own money beliefs and I don't really know what their habits around money are so some of it will be more luck than judgment. One thing is true; I won't be telling him that I want a swimming pool any time soon, besides my Mom has already put her order in with him, just in case I don't succeed. Ha! Thanks Mom.

I first started thinking about this a while back, before I had Finley in my life or Claire for that matter. My ex and I had taken her nieces to somewhere called Digger Land, it's a theme park where kids get to do fun stuff with mini JCBs. Anyway, when observing the kids on their mini diggers I found it fascinating that rather than hurtling around bashing each other with their little vehicles like me and my friends would have, the kids of today were doing something different. They were queueing for fuel at a small petrol station. Now bear in mind that these diggers didn't need fuel to move, the very act of doing something that their Moms and Dads did was more fascinating for them than the mindless violence I experienced on similar rides when I was a kid. These children were smart and essentially I started to think that this could be applied to other parts of their lives and used to teach them other important lessons primarily around finance.

When Finley was born I started right away to prepare him for the world, I started reading Mr Men books when he was literally days old, which his Mom found hilarious until recently where he is top of his class for reading but the youngest in his year. I taught him maths in the bath, making it a game rather than a chore and now I have it I am attempting to follow this on by passing this newly found financial knowledge. Think about it, what does school actually do? Teaches us all to have the same knowledge, well what gives those with the edge, the edge? It's what they know that is different to the rest and that's what I intend to give him. I remember a mate of mine at school, Pete; his Dad also called Pete owned his own business and was always up to some business or other while not wasting time thinking up new names for the family ha ha. Well as soon as Pete was old enough, he was doing the same, and did bloody well out of it too.

So what am I doing with Fin? I've started simple. Where it comes to jobs, he's already gone through the list of little boy things that they want to be when they grow up including fireman, policeman and currently artist, but to teach him about property I have used the board game monopoly, to illustrate how he could make money even while doing all of these other jobs. I've drawn attention to the fact that he is able to make money even when his piece is standing still on free parking. Other people's lives continue and so does their need to pay rent when they are 'parked' on somewhere that you own. Another thing that I have taught him to do is to pay himself (figuratively) when he lands on his own space, signifying that he is saving money by being in his own property rather than someone else's.

In addition to this, I've got him to start thinking about owning his own business and I mean contemplating the workings of an actual business. Since starting this chapter, Finley now wants to be a toy maker. We've always done crafty things and the big thing he's into at the moment is called Hama beads, you can make coasters and pictures out of these tiny plastic beads. If you're a parent these are great if you have a spare hour that you want to keep them occupied. Anyway, while we were making some coasters I got him thinking about what if we made these to sell to other people. I asked him things like how much he'd charge; £10.17 and I asked if that would cover the time we were making the beads and the materials needed. We come up with a name for the business 'Finley's Toys – Designed by Finley'. We discussed how we would package them and the next time he comes down we are going to design a box for the coasters and a poster to advertise them. This is not only fun for him to do but also gets his mind working on how to sell things and what things are worth and the whole of the marketing process. He may not end up as a toy designer or have his own business but at least he'll have some appreciation for what goes into selling a product, so at the very least he can become a better consumer.

I love Finley to bits and love doing things with him, I'm not saying to make everything about business but play can be a good way to get your kids thinking about the workings of the world.

Mom and Dad think: I'm a little bit mad trying to teach him these principles at a young age

Reality: Play is one of the key things that help you learn what to do when you're an adult, so why not start now?

CHAPTER 22 DAD AND DISNEY LAND!

Right I've left this chapter to near the end of the book as it's probably the hardest for me to write and the most personal to me and my family. When growing up my Dad worked bloody hard as a bakery engineer and for the most part he seemed to enjoy it, and still tells us about the jokes he played and funny stories and characters that he met at work. But during the 1990s it seemed that my Dad got caught up in the aspirational notion of providing the best for his family and as was the definition of being successful at the time this took the shape in the desire of taking me and my Mom to Disney Land or World or both, there wasn't a Disney Land Paris at the time so it meant a massive 'once in a life time holiday' to America.

So he did what every unleveraged working class person would do to achieve a more expensive goal.

He started to do overtime and I mean a serious amount, trading his personal time for more money but obviously losing out on time with the people he wanted to do this special thing for, me and my Mom. Now this was very noble and we were all suitably excited when we started getting the brochures to book it. However, once it was booked the effects of doing all of this overtime took its toll on us as a family. Usually, a very happy go lucky bloke he became snappy and what I can only describe as a miserable git which culminated in a fair few arguments between my parents. This unsettled environment led to the point where I made one of a very few stands against my Dad and said one night that I wouldn't talk to him if he continued the way he was towards my Mom. This shocked my Dad (and I think my Mom too if I'm honest) and he shared his desire to pay for this amazing trip for us was meaning that he had to work more when he didn't really want to be there. The truth was me and my Mom (as much as we'd have loved to go to Disney Land) we just wanted a happy time with our Dad and husband and would have foregone any holiday to have him back to his normal jolly self. Shortly after this exchange of words he reduced his overtime hours and gradually came back to the Ray that we knew and loved. We did go to America, twice actually and they were amazing holidays but looking back we had as much fun on holidays to Cornwall and Devon that probably didn't cost anywhere as near as much money.

Recently, I've noticed myself falling into this same trap occasionally; I had to have a chat with myself when Finley and Claire weren't paying attention when I was announcing a trip I had just purchased for them to Warwick Castle for Finley's birthday. I snapped saying 'well I guess it's not important that I've just spent all of this money on you pair', what the hell is that all about? As the words were leaving my mouth seeing their shocked faces the Disney debacle crashed into my mind like a bucket of ice cold water. I described my Dad as a miserable git earlier but he was like that while trying to do something special for us. What a paradox that I was now doing the same? There's an advert for a travel agent on the TV at the moment that depicts an ogre going on holiday with his family and gradually turning back into a human (their Dad!), their marketing guys have cleverly worked out that most working men are probably living for this two week period and in trying to provide the best for their family and being a good Dad is actually hard work and can making them miserable. I am currently editing this book next to Fin in the school holiday, I'm feeling guilty about that but I have promised to take him out and make up for it as soon as I'm done. Listen to the song Cats in the Cradle and you'll get the idea, my favourite version is by Ugly Kid Joe.

Mom and Dad think: Provide amazing experiences by earning more money at the expense of your time i.e. unleveraged.

Reality: Make sure you can afford your purchases and don't forsake the everyday for a two week holiday; your family appreciate your time more than your wallet!

Do what you love? Disney Part 2

I've included this in the same chapter as I think there are further parallels with my Dad and me at the moment that I want to explore. I have become more 'snappy' recently with Claire and Finley. I think that writing this book while trying to be an entrepreneur, while trying to support my family financially, while having the house sale money in the bank has confused me deeply. I can afford to quit my job, I can afford to get a buy to let property, I can afford to become a writer full time or a consultant contractor, but I don't. My Dad, could have been a plumber, he could have been a stand-up comedian he was and is one of the funniest people I've met in real life. Why didn't he? It's like work traps us. It's an illusion of security of waking up every day and having somewhere to be something to do and someone to tell us to do it. What are we and other men like me and my Dad afraid of? At the Moment I am attempting to write this book, whilst being a consultant, a Dad and a full time employee, as well as being a good friend and performing in a band. In the words of Soul Wax song Too Many DJs; 'Something's gotta give'.

I love writing, I love helping small companies, I love playing in a band, and I love life coaching. Do you love what you do? Simon Senek talks about the golden circle for success; that truly successful companies work on 'why' they do something rather than the how or what they do. I don't love the company (sorry if they're reading this) so where is my 'why'? When I worked at the Fire Service I loved it, I went there every day knowing that my existence within that company was helping people and that was my 'why', I'd go in sick and if I'm honest and I'd even have worked there for free if they'd asked me. At my current place, I like lots of the people but I mainly focus on the what, would I go there for free? Probably not, it pays me so I go and work there but that is about it. I think I know what I need to do, but will I do it?

Update: a couple of new people that I like have started and some twats have left so I'm enjoying it a lot more for now.

Mom and Dad think: I should keep my job as it's well-paid and secure.

Reality: You need to be passionate about what you do as you spend more time at work than you do at home.

CHAPTER 23
UNUSUAL BEHAVIOUR AT A CAROUSEL

This is an odd one for me, as discussed earlier, my Mom and Dad are definitely not tight and they abhor anyone that is, often cursing people in the past for being stingy or miserly. They have some hilarious phrases for tight people like 'they're so tight they've learnt how to peel an orange in their pocket' and 'they'd skin a fart for a penny'. My friend Sean at work also told me a good one from his old man which was 'if they dropped a quid, it would hit them on the back of the head on the way down' ha!

Recently, I've noticed my Dad be a bit tight but in the oddest of situations. He moaned about something that I was really surprised about. They took Fin, their grandson to the beach and while he was there, as always, he wanted to go on one of the little pay rides outside of the arcade. This time it was a carousel ride and my Dad found it outrageous that from Finley's £1 go two other children could jump on and have a 'free ride'. Wow. I challenged him on this and said 'so what?' and 'who the f*ck cares?' I was trying to say Finley gets to go on it anyway, he's not losing out if the other kids get a go at the same time and it's not as if you're going to be arsed to chase the other parents down for the respective 33p of their child is it? I was gobsmacked that someone so generous could say something so 'tight'! Anyway, he saw the error of his ways but I wonder if this frugality is spawned from retirement and having a finite budget where I'm sure he wouldn't have given a shit if the same thing had taken place when I was a little boy.

Mom and Dad think: Randomly, if you pay others shouldn't benefit.

Reality: Life's too short to worry about stuff so petty and who knows Fin may have made a little friend or two from that small investment of a quid.

CHAPTER 24
CAN'T TAKE IT WITH YOU/ NO POCKETS IN SHROUDS

For many years I had the saying 'you can't take it with you' on my lips because this is what my parents used to say to me. Technically this is a true statement but was also how I justified spending money usually on large purchases and more often than not on credit cards. This was very short sighted. This phrase and others such as 'no pockets in shrouds' always seems to be said by people justifying being frivolous or buying something big or occasionally if they had given something to somebody that was unexpected. However, when I started to read the money guru books I realise that these phrases are really just an excuse for being shit with money and mainly broke people. Yes they are right you can't take your money with you though god did the Egyptians try to albeit unsuccessfully, however the tactics listed in this book can help you to be able to at least leave some for your family.

I feel like credit cards and loans combined with technology and short termism has made people care less about the future and instead they live (and spend) for the now. Why can't we stop making that massive purchase that we can't really afford? Why do we need a new car when our old one is barely two years old? Who are we trying to impress or prove something to? I feel like consumerism has come round full circle and now no one steals any-thing because everyone has everything! Sorry for that random rant.

If this is your phrase and you're broke you need to start showing some self-restraint. Resist the ad-verts, newsflash David Beckham doesn't wear David Beckham aftershave cause he wants to smell good and probably wears some posher shit than we'll ever be able to afford because he can afford it be-cause us morons are buying his shit aftershave. Also, guess what? Someone who can afford a Polo jumper doesn't buy a pissing jumper with Polo plastered all over it because they can afford the one that doesn't have it plastered all over it and don't need to prove that they can afford a Polo jumper by having the name f*cking plastered all over it.

Enough of the 'no pockets in shrouds', it's kind of like the reverse of 'saving for a rainy day', can't we just invent a new phrase like 'invest some, spend some, keep some' or 'don't hoard it but don't piss it up the wall either'.

Mom and Dad think: You can't take it with you

Reality: You can leave a legacy.

CHAPTER 25
MONEY CAN'T
BUY YOU
HAPPINESS

This is another stock phrase of the eternally broke, the money masters testify that money can't buy you happiness or love, but I bet its loads better to be sad and lonely in a mansion with a Ferrari than in a flat without even f*cking bus fare to get to Poundland! This is up there with 'pockets in shrouds' and 'can't take it with you'. If you really look at these, they're just excuses to justify not having any money. If you think about the earlier chapter about positive thinking, what are these thoughts and phrases manifesting? That you don't want nor need money because you're not going to take it with you and you'll be happy without it, f*ck that.

Newsflash people, if you have no money then that's your own fault no one else's, it's not your parents or your teachers or the fact you were bullied it's yours. You are spending more than you earn bit like people eating more than they exercise and blaming their genes or metabolism. As you're born there's not an invisible label stuck on you saying 'broke' and others saying 'rich' or 'comfortable' or 'fat' or 'thin'. Stop making excuses using these phrases and do something to change your life, go to a class, learn a trade, don't buy that random item, believe you can attract money and it will come.

Universe if you're listening, I'm taking it with me and I'll only be happy with loads of it! Thanks.

How many of these phrases do you or your family have that have been passed down the generations? Can you reprogram your thoughts to be more helpful rather than making excuses for the fact you can't exercise self-restraint? If you can I truly believe that your financial situation will improve.

Quick random rant, I think the term 'benefits' is a terrible name for what they actually are. Benefit is a positive word; I'd like some benefits in my life. If they called it 'loser money' or 'skint handout' less people would probably claim and work out how to avoid the stigma of collecting it.

Mom and Dad think: Money doesn't buy you happiness.

Reality: How do they know it can't, if they've never had loads of it?

CHAPTER 26
SO WHAT HAVE
I BECOME?
(CONCLUSION)

Well what a journey through the past right up until present day this book has been for me. I did not make the deadline of the end of my honeymoon but I definitely moved quicker on this than anything else I've ever done in my life. Some of this was hard to write and some of it was great to recollect, I hope my Mom and Dad know that I love them to pieces and that anything written in this book is to help, guide and support people who want to improve their financial situation and not to dig at them. And I also hope they appreciate that it's only my view of the world and absolutely loved my childhood which probably (if I'm honest) lasted far too long into my 20s maybe even 30s.

Now I've 'grown up' and I have learnt some of the tips of the richest people in the world (albeit vicariously) I feel I have a good foundation from both worlds, i.e. being frugal and saving as well as being brave enough to do what my parents and their peers didn't which is to invest my time and money into the world rather than getting one job and saving money at all costs, sometimes at the expense of my free time and in other instances at the expense of relationships. I still look for a bargain or if there's any cashback (topcashback.co.uk) on a purchase but at the same time take calculated risks with my money in order to achieve higher gains than a standard savings account. I still have my job trading time for money which I really need to think long and hard about whether it's right for me long term or not.

The moral of the story though I'm not sure that I really need one, is when you say something as parents, grandparents to your children and loved ones the listener receiving the information may hold what you say to be true and can strongly influence their financial situation as well as their children and others around them. By the same token what is said to you can influence your views and you have the power to challenge and reject the advice even it is said by someone that you love dearly. The people passing on the advice have different needs, wants, desires and importantly tolerance to risk and we need to keep that in mind when it comes to money matters. All decisions have a 50/50 chance of working out so be careful of what you hold to be the right advice and the impact that your 'truth' can affect your friends and family. My parents loved me unconditionally which I am forever grateful for, their belief system was my reality for a massive chunk of my life, and if they'd have chosen to, this could have been their belief in religion, football teams etc. so please respect the power that you have and just go easy when sharing your views unless you're Martin Lewis, then fill your boots as you know you're stuff.

Remember, just because you love someone doesn't mean you have to believe everything that they say or vice versa. Your thoughts and attitude affect your situation directly, you are in control of your life you just have to believe it and be careful how much of your values are your own. In other words check who's advice you're taking if they're not in a situation you want to be in it may not be the best course of action.

My final thought like Jerry Springer, is as follows; does risk aversion come with age? Will I eventually be telling my kids to invest in less risky things and to save for a 'rainy day'? Will they be looking at me thinking I need to expand my money horizons? Well future me, if you're reading this as I haven't got a time travelling Delorean to come and tell you to keep your mind open and take calculated risks but I do have this book and if you've just read it now you're 60 plus go and sort yourself out and get your money out those bloody Premium Bonds!

Thanks for reading, I hope you enjoyed it and found

it useful as much as I did by writing it.

Peace out AJ1 aka Son of Nette and Bastard Face.

The moral right of Adam Jones to be indentified as the author of this work has been asserted in accordance with the Copyright, Designs and Patent Act 1988

Copyright (c) 2019 Adam Jones

37147298R00078

Printed in Poland
by Amazon Fulfillment
Poland Sp. z o.o., Wrocław